To Don:

Happy Belated Birthday!
(Better late than Never) ☺

Tee. 2003

The Science of Feng Shui

7/10/2002

©2002 Times Media Private Limited

Published by Times Books International
an imprint of Times Media Private Limited
Times Centre, 1 New Industrial Road, Singapore 536196
Tel: (65) 6213 9288 Fax: (65) 6285 4871
Email: te@tpl.com.sg
Online Bookstore: http://www.timesone.com.sg/te

Times Subang
Lot 46, Subang Hi-Tech Industrial Park, Batu Tiga
40000 Shah Alam, Selangor Darul Ehsan, Malaysia
Tel & Fax: (603) 5636 3517
Email: cchong@tpg.com.my

Cosmic digital illustrations created by Roi Hew
Photographs by C.P. Lim

Printed in Singapore

National Library Board (Singapore) Cataloguing in Publication Data

Lim, C. P.
The science of feng shui : the oriental scientific way to perfect your environment / C.P. Lim. –
Singapore : Times Books International, c2002.
     p. cm.
     ISBN : 981-232-179-9

1.   Feng shui. I. Title.

BF1779.F4
133.3337 — dc21   SLS2002024982

The Science of Feng Shui

The Oriental scientific way to perfect your environment...

cp Lim

TIMES BOOKS INTERNATIONAL
Singapore • Kuala Lumpur

Starting your day with a smile

...This book covers most of C.P. Lim's intended PhD research topic — the cosmic environment and mankind. C.P. Lim wanted it to be a source of indepth information on feng shui and the modern environment. Although the PhD programme did not take place, C.P. Lim's research on the topic never ceased...

— Dr. Li Heng Lih

仁者見之謂之仁

知者見之謂之知

百姓日用而不知

故君子之道鮮矣

Foreword

李亨利哲学博士

Dr. Li Heng Lih

President, International Institute of Tao Philosophy

$\mathcal{F}$eng shui is an ancient science of oriental origin in which the balance of magnetic forces are sought. It has remained in existence for more than 5,000 years. In the olden days, this skill was only practised by the imperial architects. It was not until much later that feng shui was practised in civilian architecture.

The practice of feng shui begins with I-Ching's philosophy of balance. This theory relates largely to the principle of the yin and yang forces. The study of these forces involved the humanitarian, architectural and immediate environment used by human beings. The balance of the inner physical force and the environmental forces became the most important aspect of feng shui applications. It was because of this practice that the Chinese were very particular about their ancestral burial grounds and space for the living. This has been practised for many generations, and it eventually developed into one of the most remarkable philosophical studies in oriental culture.

C.P. Lim's interest in feng shui began in his early school days. He learnt card fortune telling and zodiac astrology from books. It was in the late 1980s that I met him at one of my I-Ching seminars in Singapore. That was when he enrolled himself as my student. Since then, he has learnt I-Ching, the Art of War, Fate and Fortune of the Eight Pillars, Zi Wei Dou Shu, Qi Men, pgysiognomy, theology and geomancy from me. These lessons spanned more than 14 years and during the later years, he wrote a number of articles and published three books in Chinese. Many of my students write and publish their feng shui books in Chinese and I had always hoped that some of them would publish books in English so that we can share this knowledge with feng shui enthusiasts who cannot read Chinese. I was indeed very pleased to learn that C.P. Lim will be publishing his fourth book in English. This book covers most of C.P. Lim's intended PhD research topic — the cosmic environment and mankind. C.P. Lim wanted it to be a source of indepth information on feng shui and the modern environment. Although the PhD programme did not take place, C.P. Lim's research on the topic never ceased. It gives me great pleasure to wish C.P. Lim every success in his research in feng shui.

Li Heng Lih

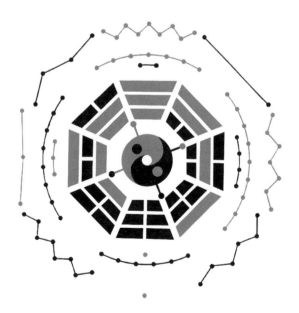

This book is delicated to
my teacher Dr. Li Heng Lih
for his many years of patience
in imparting his knowledge to me.

Contents

Introduction

$\mathcal{F}$eng shui (风水) is the art of environmental studies relating to the magnetic forces within the universe. For more than 5,000 years, the Chinese developed and practised this philosophy. There has been no specific western term to describe this practice, but the Chinese term *feng shui* is commonly used. It is also known as *geomancy*.

The most direct interpretation of the term feng shui is *wind* for *feng* and *water* for *shui*. In the practise of geomancy, these are the two main elements believed to create harmony and balance within an environment.

Geomancy started with no specific intention nor was it invented by a single person. It had its roots millions of years ago when upright apes went in search of the most suitable living environment. Through the ages, this divine study gradually became theologically inclined and at one time, there was so much mysticism involved that its theology could not be explained scientifically.

In the beginning, it was for survival that man started to look for environments that provided for their most fundamental needs such as food, water and safe shelter. These were the basic necessities for life. Gradually, the need to balance living conditions began to draw man's attention when he noticed changes in the atmosphere. There was light and darkness within a day and warm and cold weathers at different times of the year. The need to cope with these conditions began to take importance. Man learnt to prepare for and overcome unforeseen circumstances. Eventually, the fundamental principles of survival (feng shui) began to move away from basic living requirements towards becoming a means of achieving wealth and prosperity.

During the imperial era, there were some principles of feng shui that were only practised and developed by the imperial rulers. The emperor believed that imperial buildings founded on auspicious grounds would make his empire prosperous and his people would be able to share of the wealth sent from heaven. As such, these feng shui methods were restricted for use within the imperial palace and tombs of the royal family.

For generations, the commoners were unaware of these methods of feng shui and their effects. However, some of the theories required the employment of factors beyond the imperial grounds. There were also certain theories that were clearly exhibited in the imperial architecture. It was from these guidelines that the civilians began to learn the fundamental principles of feng shui.

Today, most people still believe that a building located southeast and facing northwest will give rise to scholars and descendants of great skill. A building located directly north and facing south will bring rulers in the next generation as the imperial palaces were so located for many generations. As this was believed to be the source of power to create emperors during the imperial era, civilians aligning their dwellings in this direction could be charged for attempting to overthrow the emperor. Thus, the feng shui methods permitted for use by the civilians were restricted to those that would bring good health and skills to the community as a whole. The practise of theories that were believed to develop personal wealth was prohibited. These restrictions were also applied to burials. It was believed that there were certain orientations, measurements of tombs and choice of burials grounds that held the power to bring wealth and status to the family's descendants.

The practice of feng shui was believed to have been fully revealed to the civilians only during the age of the Warring States (403–221 B.C.). The scripts were smuggled out of the imperial library by an imperial geomancer, Yang Yunsong (杨韵松). Yang left the palace amidst the confusion of the war with most of the imperial feng shui scripts which he had written. He was later given the name Jiuping (救贫) meaning "help the poor". Yang's knowledge of feng shui began to spread openly. This resulted in the development of many different methods which gradually

came under different clans due to the different living environments, customs and habits in the various provinces of China.

As a result, modern feng shui practitioners were faced with many difficulties as some of the theories used were so complex that no practitioner seemed to be able to discern the correct method for a specific application. In many cases, a method which was supposed to be employed for hilly lands was actually being applied to a coastal zone. The method for magnetic field allocations was also being enforced into environments regardless of its surroundings, which are the fundamentals of the theory. The application of feng shui became ineffective and people began to have doubts about it.

To better understand the original theories, people began to look to the Chinese imperial encyclopedia, the *Imperial Si Ku Quan Shu* (钦定四库全书) where the imperial methods of feng shui were recorded. This encyclopedia is the largest single title publication in history, consisting over 1,500 volumes. These records became the fundamental guideline for the development of oriental culture all over the world.

The complexity of feng shui applications, however, resulted in many geomancers creating simplified methods of practice. Some of these methods are said to be classified clan secrets and are not to be disclosed to outsiders. As a result, feng shui once again became something of a mystery. Despite this, the imperial records of feng shui methodologies will be the living guideline for feng shui practitioners for many more generations to come. In the imperial encyclopedia, the practice of feng shui was classified within one of the five schools of Oriental culture under the section *Feature* (相学). Although the five schools were interrelated, each of the sections maintained its individual philosophy. They were derived from the yin (阴) and yang (阳) theories of I-Ching philosophy where the ultimate objective was to establish a balance among the environmental magnetic forces. The five schools cover the key aspects of Oriental culture from medical to astrological studies.

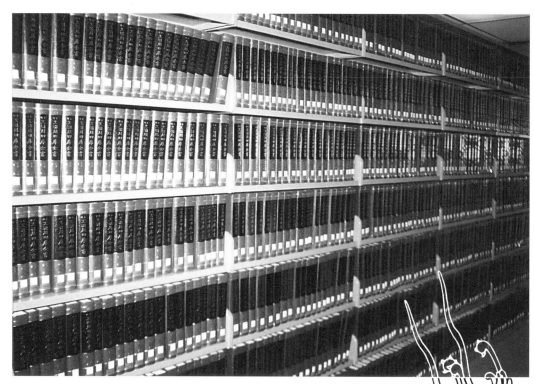

The Imperial Si Ku Quan Shu (钦定四库全书) is the largest single title publication in history.

五千年的文化将永远与人类共存 …
5,000 years of culture lives on …

Chapter 1
The Five Schools 五术

The five schools cover the key aspects of traditional Chinese cultural studies. They are the philosophical (山), medical (医), fate (命), prediction (卜) and feature (相) schools.

The philosophical school comprises the thoughts and teachings of Lao Zi (老子) and Zhuang Zi (庄子). They were profound Chinese philosophers in the study of mankind and nature. Other studies such as physical health, martial arts and the use of charms are also part of this group. The medical school deals mainly with healing, acupuncture and medical prescriptions. The fate school consists of horoscope studies, Four Pillars astrology (四柱推命) and Zi Wei Dou Shu (紫微斗数). These are mainly related to the study of life based on one's birth details. The prediction school consists of the study of the Tai Yi mystical numbers (太乙神数), Qi Men (奇门遁甲), Da Liu Ren (大六壬) and Duan Yi (断易). These studies are based mainly on the numerical principles used to reveal one's past and future. The feature school comprises the visual elements of burial grounds (风水), architecture (阳宅), physionomy and palm reading (手与面相), appellation (姓名学) and Chinese seal impressions (印文学). The study of feng shui belongs to this group as its basic philosophy is based on the effect of the burial ground on the deceased and the ideal architectural environment for the living.

The five schools became the fundamental guide to living for the Chinese for over 5,000 years. The complexity of the contents of the five schools makes it very difficult for any individual to master all of them. Throughout its history, there were masters specialised in only one or two of the five groups. The practise of some of the theories requires one to be in specific locations. For example, the meditation and practise of charms require one to be nearer to the natural environment such as a mountainside, stream or waterfall in order to achieve maximum effect. Thus, the practise of each group is very specific.

There was a sixth practice that is not classified within the five schools. This is the theological group. Due to its mystical contents, it was classified as a supernatural culture with factors that are beyond modern day science. In this practice, individual practitioners perform mystical healings in various ways. In most cases, healing is done in the presence of an altar and other related objects to achieve extreme effects. This practice is sometimes referred to as black magic. In modern feng shui, the use of charms, crystals or talismans are all derived from the theological group. The objects utilised and the methods applied are believed to be capable of generating psychological effects from the internal magnetic fields. They achieve effects that are beyond explanation.

The Five Schools

| 山 | 医 | 命 | 卜 | 相 |
Philosophical	Medical	Fate	Prediction	Feature
Talismans & Charms Martial Arts & Meditation Philosophy of Zhuang Zi Philosophy of Lao Zi Diet & Health	Healing Acupuncture Prescription	Horoscope Four Pillars Zi Wei Dou Shu	Tai Yi Mystical Numbers Qi Men Liu Ren Duan Yi	Feng Shui Architecture Physiognomy & Palm Reading Appellation Seal Impression

The sixth practice was not classified
under the five schools. This was
due to the inherent mysticism
which could not be proven
by science. They are ...

the supernatural culture

with factors beyond

modern day science.

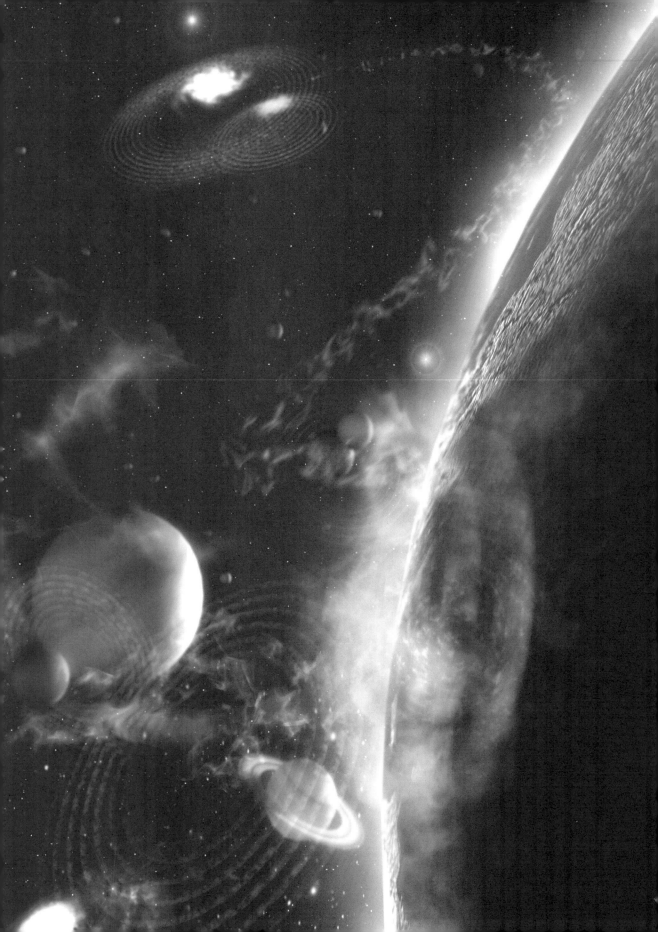

Chapter 2
The Environmental Force
Qi (Chi) 氕

The modern Chinese word for *chi* (气) is *qi*. Qi refers to the cosmic forces that are generated through the movements of the heavenly bodies within the universe. In travelling through the universe, the force expands and contracts. It creates turbulence when it reaches earth's atmosphere. It turns into energy and wind when arriving at the earth's surface and coming into contact with three dimensional objects and uneven surfaces. It changes its course when it encounters warm or cold environments.

The conditions on earth allow qi to travel in a straight line, in circular motion or in any form and any way. It creates hurricanes and storms. It brings with it certain elements that control the inner and outer space of the human being. Qi is an element that humans can only try to find ways of living around rather than going against.

Types of Wind

The movements of qi transforms into various forms of wind when it comes in contact with the earth's surface. The three main types of wind are contour wind (地形风), pressure wind (气压风) and cosmic wind (自转风). Each takes on different characteristics at different times and at different locations.

Contour wind occurs when qi comes into contact with three dimensional objects such as buildings, mountains and trees. Pressure wind occurs when qi comes into contact with warm or cold air. The expansion or contraction of pressure wind creates movements that turn into primary wind and if it comes into contact with any object, it will become contour wind.

The third form of wind, cosmic wind is created by the revolving action of the earth. As the earth revolves, it creates a cycle of moving forces. When these forces travel into outer space, they run into the pressures created by the movement of the planets. This impact eventually transforms into a form of cosmic air movement. When these movements come into earth's atmosphere, they create cosmic wind. Cosmic wind may come into earth's atmosphere mild or extremely rough. As the latter, it will cause hurricanes or ocean storms. The atmospheric forces resulting from these movements affect qi. These effects could be felt over a wide area or within a confined space. It may affect an entire city, a whole village or just a single building. It is because of this uncertainty that some feng shui applications may not be effective. Apart from the atmospheric conditions, the periodical weather changes and climatic differences also play a considerable role. The force travelling through these zones from east to west or from north to south may undergo drastic changes due to the different weather conditions. These changes may affect an entire zone or just a small area. They could affect an entire housing estate or just the rooms inside a building. These forces present mankind with a wide spectrum of uncertainty.

The five schools comprise a wide range of physical practices and qi remains the main influencing factor. In Oriental culture, ensuring the balance among one's immediate living surroundings, the burial ground and properties to be handed down to future generations became the main concerns of living. It was believed that only when a person is able to achieve a balance in the environmental forces for at least three generations to come, will he be able to make good in his next life. It was also a believed that a person could be reincarnated into his own family. Thus, the need to provide for future generations became an important criteria of life. These beliefs and practices have existed for many generations. The teaching and thoughts of Confucius (孔子), Lao Zi and Zhuang Zi, which were based mainly on the inner and outer forces (qi), became the philosophy of living in Oriental culture.

Types of Qi

The environmental forces (qi) in feng shui are manifested in three forms. They are the architectural force (宅气), human force (人气) and object force (物气). They are known as the three positive forces (阳宅三气). It is the balance among these three forces that determines whether the feng shui in a specific area is good or bad.

The architectural force refers to the appearance of a building in relation to its environment. It is important to ensure that new buildings complement the other buildings in the same area. Good feng shui will not be achieved if a residential building is situated in a slump area or close to industrial zones. Feng shui practitioners believe that such buildings will not bring prosperity to its occupants. Instead, they may be plagued with illnesses and worries.

The human force refers to the human relationships present within a building. Negative forces tend to develop due to the lack of mutual understanding and respect among people who occupy the building. The negative human forces could sometimes also be due to the negative architectural forces in the surroundings. It is therefore important to ensure that there are positive forces within a radius of at least 5 km to achieve good feng shui. The wider the positive zone, the better the feng shui.

Object force refers to the interior of a building. In this respect, all furniture and fixtures within the building must be maintained in proper condition at all times. This will help ensure that the object force is kept positive. Broken furniture or loose hinges should be fixed. Old and unused kitchen utensils or clothing should be cleared. Items which have not been used for more than two years must also be discarded or its qi will deteriorate and affect the qi of other objects around it. Similarly, aquariums, ponds or household pets must be kept clean and healthy. All movable items within a single household must also not occupy more than 60 percent of the total floor area. In other words, there should be at least 40 percent of free space with the exception of industrial warehouses. These three positive forces are the fundamental elements to maintaining good feng shui.

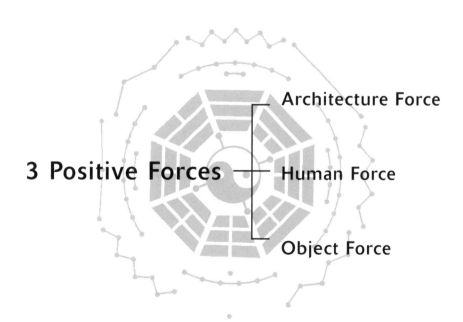

3 Positive Forces — Architecture Force / Human Force / Object Force

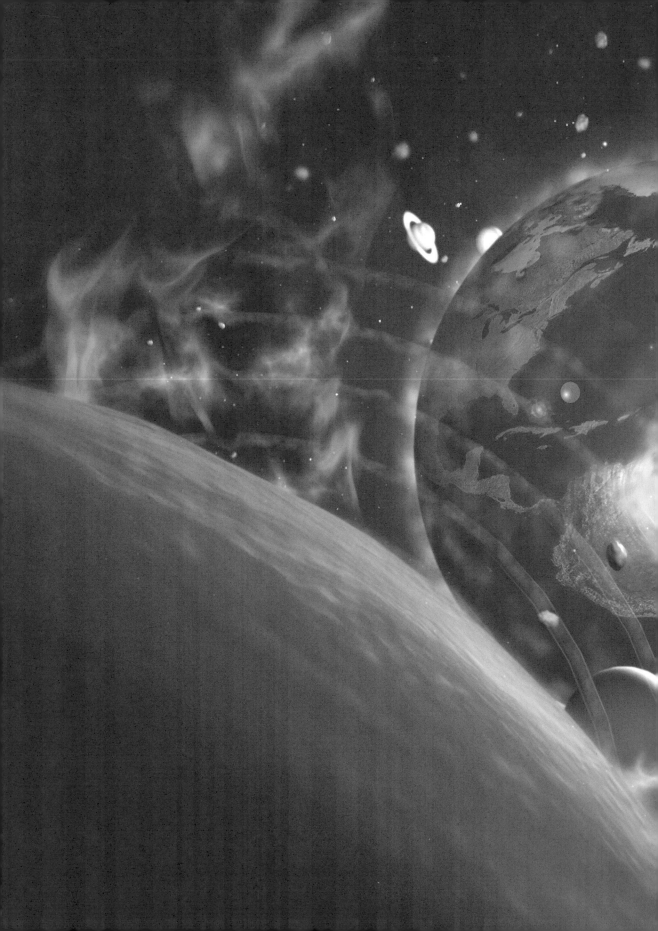

Chapter 3
The Universal Force

The three environmental forces — the architecture force, the human force and the object force — are extensions of the universal magnetic fields known as the cosmic force. They begin in outer space. They are created by the movement of the planets near the earth. These movements gradually affect the earth and all its inhabitants.

Early feng shui masters managed to relate these forces with a set of numbers known as the He Tu (河图) and Luo Shu (洛书) numbers. These numbers were later related to the stars in the northern hemisphere which are known as the Big Dipper. The position of these stars are the magnetic forces that relate to most changes on earth.

The position of each star coincides with all other numerical principles applied in fate and fortune philosophy. The numbers are also related to the cycles of the sun, earth and moon. They represent the 12-month cycle of each calendar year and relates to the date and time of an individual's birth. Each relationship further creates a formula that when combined with the yin and yang philosophy, makes it possible to foretell the future of an individual

and the environment. These concepts will be discussed in the later chapters of this book.

The magnetic fields from outer space are the main factors that shape the earth's surface. These magnetic fields are transmitted on a massive scale from outer space to earth. They transform into forces and will encounter obstacles that will change them. As a result, different locations on earth will receive different forces and experience different outcomes. The effects on the earth's surface might take months, years or an even longer period before they become visible. Some of the forces travel through mountains and

valleys, some through cities with high rise buildings and some through open fields in the country. The force that travels into the

mountain ranges was known as dragon lair (also dragon or dragon force) to the ancients. The dragon lair refers the contour patterns formed by a group of mountains or mountain ranges. The force travelling through the valleys is believed to be the most powerful and natural. It has the ability of changing the ego force of an individual (*Chapter 4: Good and Bad Feng Shui*). Between the valley contours, there are points known as Xue (穴) and Mai (脉). These points are believed to have hidden forces that can effect changes for at least three future generations. The ancient feng shui masters would earnestly locate these points for burial purposes.

The magnetic forces moving among the mountain ranges move in the same way as symbolised by the mystical dragon. The mystical dragon bears the characteristics of a few auspicious creatures believed to have the power of bringing good fortune to people. It has the horns of a deer, the eyes and whiskers of a carp, the nose and ears of a cow, the paws of a tiger, the claws of an eagle, the body of a snake, the scales of a fish and the mouth of a kirin. Dragon lair became the fundamental guideline to locating spots endowed with

good feng shui. The same principle was also related to roads, rivers and streams that flowed within the land and around the geographical contours. Human fate, fortune, wealth and health are believed to be dependent on the flow of these magnetic forces.

These magnetic forces that flow around the valleys, mountain ranges, roads and rivers, however, have different effects on the environment. There are auspicious and inauspicious flows. They can be classified as steep flows, level flows and direct flows.

Steep flows come from higher ground. Level flows move on flat surface ground. Direct flows come in from a steep bend round the back of a mountain or a tall building. To identify whether the flows are auspicious or inauspicious, the ground level conditions in the area will have to be studied. The study should cover an area that is at least 5 km wide. The ideal flows are the level ones that end in the sea or continue into a larger group of mountain ranges or low land contours. The effect of the magnetic forces that flow around

low rise or tall buildings, however, are not as distinct unless the building is situated within the flow path of other magnetic forces.

Domestic feng shui is dependent on the surroundings of the building as well as its interior. The feng shui principles applied for the interior of a house will not be appropriate if it does not relate to the magnetic flows of the surrounding land contours. It must also be recognised that these land contours do not just end at the edge of the sea. They continue

The land contours do not end at the edge of the sea. They continue into the water.

Effective Feng Shui can only be established from studying the surrounding area not less than 5 km wide.

into the water and connect to other lands. Thus, the study of the surrounding areas is important in order to apply the principles of feng shui effectively. Feng shui studies must also relate to the five elements of wood, fire, earth, metal and water (*Chapter 4: Five Elements*). The importance of environmental energies and their relationship with the He Tu and Luo Shu numbers became the basis of feng shui principles.

The mystical dragon symbolises the mountain ranges on earth.

The Nine Flying Stars and the Magic Numbers

The numerical logics applied in feng shui were developed with reference to the Big Dipper, a group of stars in the northern hemisphere. Two stars were added to the left and the right of the seven star group, forming the Nine Flying Stars (also known as the Nine Star Force or the Northern Scoop Stars). The ancient feng shui masters created a nine square grid for the Nine Flying Stars to visualise the relationship of the compass directions and the magnetic forces. This set of numbers outline the path of the stars and correspond to the numbers of the Luo Shu. They are also known as the magic numbers of the universe.

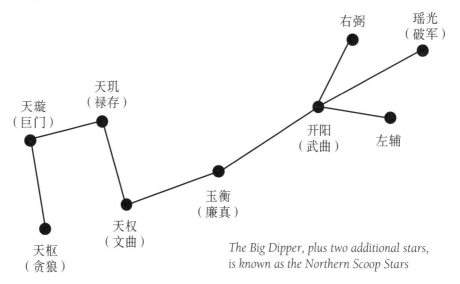

右弼

瑶光
（破军）

天玑
（禄存）

天璇
（巨门）

开阳
（武曲）

左辅

天权
（文曲）

玉衡
（廉真）

天枢
（贪狼）

The Big Dipper, plus two additional stars, is known as the Northern Scoop Stars

4	9	2
3	5	7
8	1	6

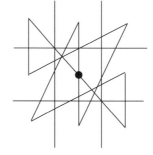

SE	S	SW
E	☯	W
NE	N	NW

The placement of the numbers within the grid.

The running sequence of the numbers correspond to the path of the stars.

The compass directions within the grid.

The number nine is the largest in numerical principle. It has been referred to as the heavenly figure. It is positioned at the top of the nine star grid for this reason. Number one, on the other hand is man's figure. It can be said to be the smallest number and also the largest. It is placed at the bottom section of the nine square grid. In running sequence, the number five is the middle figure. It is referred to as the earth figure and sits in the middle of the grid. Each of these numbers is related to the five elements. The diagram below shows the numbers and their corresponding element.

1 2 3 4 [5] 6 7 8 9

9 - Heaven 天

---

5 - Earth 地

---

1 - Man 人

Chapter 4
Yin & Yang Philosophy

The knowledge of positive and negative forces were believed to have been observed by an ancient sage known as Fu Xi (伏牺). These are all recorded in the I-Ching scripts. Sage Fu Xi observed the changes in the heavens and on earth. He contemplated the relationship of the earth with its creatures and with man.

It was through these observations that sage Fu Xi began to construct the ba gua (八卦). It was the first set of symbols that signified the balance between the positive and negative forces in the universe. The discovery of this yin (negative) and yang (positive) philosophy became the fundamental element in feng shui studies up to the present day.

古包牺氏之王天下也。仰则观象於天。
府则观法於地。观鸟兽之文。与地之宜。
近取诸身。远取诸物。於是始作八卦。

Yang   **Yin**

Tai Chi

Sage Fu Xi

The Tai Chi Symbol

The symbol for yin is a broken line and for yang a solid line. These are also the symbols that differentiate male and female, masculine and feminine, weak and strong and hot and cold. The yin and yang philosophy was later developed into the pictorial symbol of the tai chi.

The tai chi symbol consists of an equal black (yin) and white (yang) portion. The shape of both portions resemble a circular moving action which signifies the continuous changes of universal forces and their influence on the living environment. Within the yin, there is a bit of yang and within the yang, there is a bit of yin. This symbolises the interrelationship of the two. The tai chi symbol became the symbolic image representing all forms of changes including day and night, hot and cold seasons and life and death.

**Wu Chi
Emptiness**

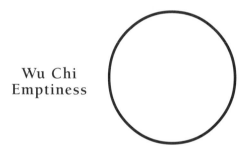

In the early days, it was thought that man's existence helped balance the forces between heaven and earth. The early tai chi symbol represented this belief with a circle sumbolic of emptiness (wu chi).

Heaven

Man

Earth

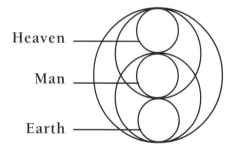

Within it were three smaller circles of equal size. The circle on top represented heaven, the bottom one represented earth and the middle one represented man.

The black and white sections represented the magnetic forces that circulate the space around man.

Day

Night

These forces included day and night...

Heaven

Earth

...heaven and earth...

Summer

Spring

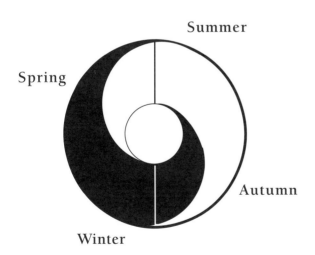

Autumn

Winter

...the four seasons...

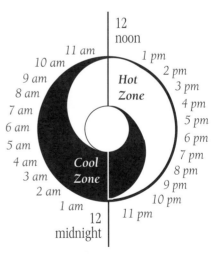

...and the 24 hours of a day.

Early tai chi symbol.

Modern day tai chi symbol.

The modern tai chi symbol evolved with the gradual realisation that heaven and earth were the two main controlling forces and that man was neither equal to heaven nor to earth. Thus, the tai chi symbol today represents these two major forces of heaven (yang) and earth (yin). Man is no longer represented within the symbol.

The development of tai chi and ba gua

Wu Chi (Emptiness)   Tai Chi (Movement)

Yang   **Yin**

Four Main Directions

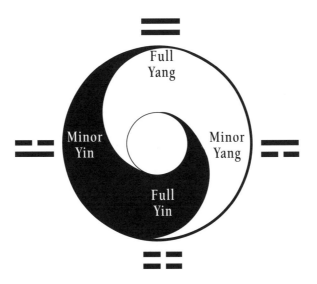

Full
Yang

Minor
Yin

Minor
Yang

Full
Yin

The Eight Trigram

1	2	3	4	5	6	7	8
Heaven	Lake	Fire	Thunder	Wind	Water	Mountain	Earth

It was from sage Fu Xi's studies that the fundamental philosophy for the development of the eight trigram or ba gua (八卦) came about. The ba gua incorporates the primary and secondary compass directions — north, south, east, west, northwest, northeast, southwest and southeast.

There were a number of different ba gua developed in history, but Fu Xi's ba gua, known as the Heavenly ba gua, was the first group of symbols to represent the atmospheric and geographic conditions of earth. The patterns in this ba gua represent the eight universal elements of heaven, earth,

fire, water, lake, wind, thunder and mountain. The position of each element is significant. Each one faces a directly opposing element. For example, water faces fire, heaven faces earth, mountain faces lake and wind faces thunder. These elements are believed to be in balance and the Chinese use the ba gua as a reference to balance the magnetic forces in the living environment.

The ba gua is usually placed outside, above the front door of the house. It is believed that a ba gua hung outside the house has the power to deflect unpleasant elements and prevent negative forces from entering.

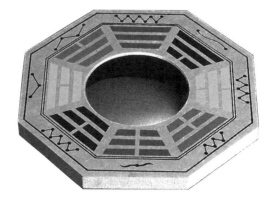

The modern day Heavenly ba gua is used to prevent negative forces from entering the home.

The ba gua incense burner.

A marble ba gua.

Modern Ba Gua

Today, the ba gua comes in a variety of designs. There are those imprinted with scripture, patterns of altars, tiger heads, the positions of the northern cosmic stars as well as those fitted with mirrors.

Among the various designs, the tiger head ba gua is considered to be the most aggressive ba gua with the power to deflect unpleasant forces to the extent of destroying and eliminating them. Due to its extreme power, this type of ba gua is not suitable for use in domestic dwellings. It is used mainly for commercial buildings, farms, schools, temples and military grounds. Apart from the tiger head ba gua, all other types of ba gua may be used for the home.

The pictures of the ba gua shown here all have the element of heaven represented

The ba gua with a tiger head is not suitable for use in domestic dwellings.

by three yang strokes (solid lines) at the top. They are known as the Heavenly ba gua. They are usually hung in an upright position above the entrance of a building. The Heavenly ba gua may also be reproduced on the floor of religious institutions. It is believed that religious institutions are visited by different types of people with different characters. Thus, having the Heavenly ba gua on the floor will eliminate the negative forces in each person as they pass through to enter into the inner hall of the building.

The Heavenly ba gua.

The other type of ba gua with a yin stroke in the middle of two yang strokes at the top is not suitable for use as a device to balance the magnetic forces. Known as the Earthly ba gua, it is only used as a compass to determine the direction that a building should face or if a location requires the application of feng shui. It is very important not to confuse the Heavenly ba gua and the Earthly ba gua, given their different effects and uses.

There are other types of ba gua recorded in history. Many of them, however, are no longer in use today as the ba gua needs to be changed to suit the changing customs and needs of people.

The Earthly ba gua.

The ba gua on the floor of religious buildings.

He Tu 河图 and Luo Shu 洛书

He Tu (river diagram) and Luo Shu (book of Luo) were two major discoveries in the history of Chinese Metaphysical Studies.

He Tu

Recorded in the I-Ching, He Tu may be understood as the *mystic patterns from the river*. Sage Fu Xi spotted a mystical dragon horse rising from the Yellow River with markings on its back. These markings became known as He Tu.

The arrangement of the trigrams in the Heavenly ba gua were derived from these mystical patterns. He Tu was later developed to become a very powerful tool for divination. It was combined with compass directions and the five elements.

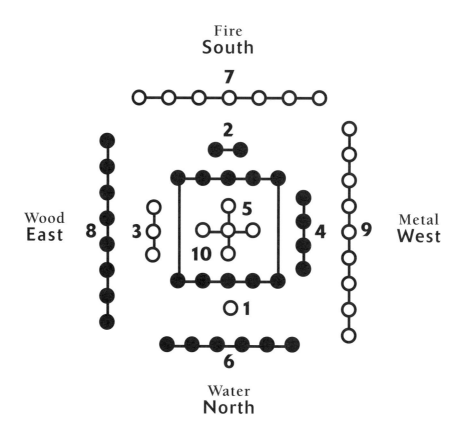

The arrangement of the trigrams on the Heavenly ba gua were developed from the markings on the back of the dragon horse.

The dragon horse observed by sage Fu Xi.

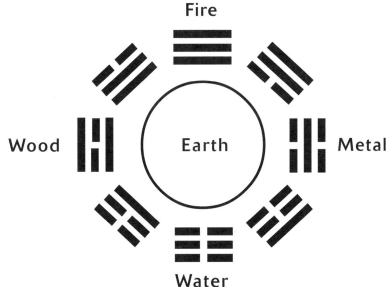

Fire

Wood   Earth   Metal

Water

The Heavenly ba gua is related to the order of the five elements.

Luo Shu

Luo Shu can be understood as the *inscriptions from the Luo province*. It was discovered during the floods that plagued the Xia dynasty (circa 1600 B.C.). The architect who managed the flood outburst was the ruler, Da Yu (大禹).

During one of his missions to manage a flood at the Yellow River, he spotted a dragon tortoise with a set of mystical inscriptions on its shell. The order of these inscriptions were different from those found from the dragon horse. These markings were known as the Luo numbers. They were later developed by Emperor Wen during the Shang dynasty (1600–1100 B.C.).

The numerical orders of both the Heavenly and the Earthly ba gua were related to the five elements. The difference between them is that the Heavenly ba gua comprises the complementary orders of the five elements when they move in a clockwise direction, whereas the Earthly ba gua comprises the conflicting orders of the five elements when they move in an anti-clockwise direction. These two orders became the major reference for the magnetic force feng shui method (理气风水法) commonly practised today.

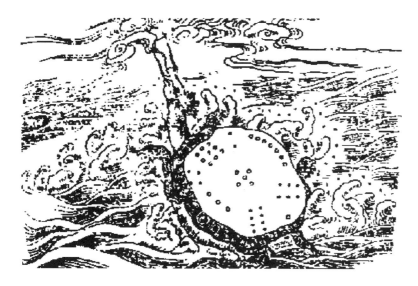

The dragon tortoise spotted by Da Yu.

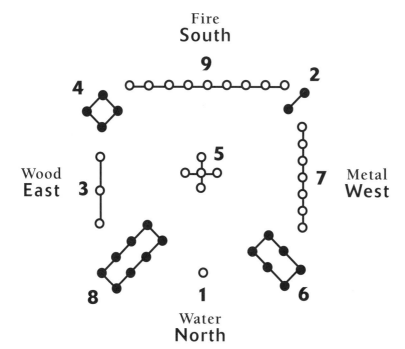

The mystical inscriptions on the shell of the dragon tortoise was instrumental in the development of the Earthly ba gua.

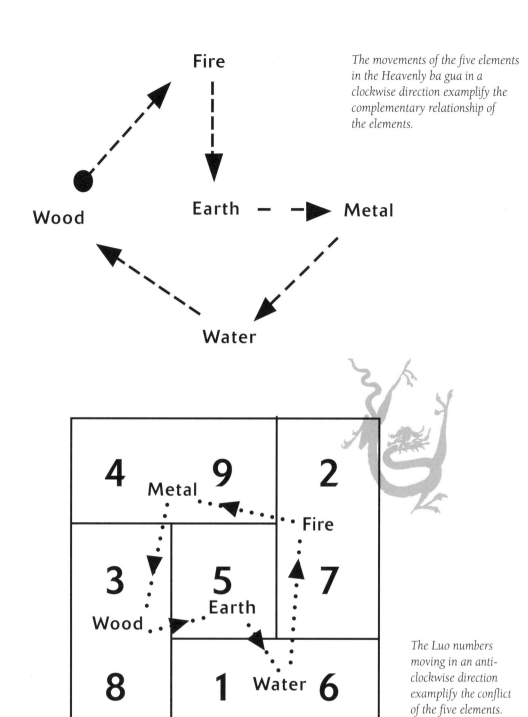

Fire

Wood

Earth — → Metal

Water

The movements of the five elements in the Heavenly ba gua in a clockwise direction examplify the complementary relationship of the elements.

4	9	2
Metal		Fire
3	5	7
Wood	Earth	
8	1 Water	6

The Luo numbers moving in an anti-clockwise direction examplify the conflict of the five elements.

The dragon tortoise

Five Elements

The five elements refer to the five universal elements of wood, fire, earth, metal and water. These five elements are believed to be constantly interacting with one another. There are in fact two cyclical relationships that these elements are involved in. They are the cycle of complements and the cycle of conflicts.

The cycle of complements exhibits the natural characteristics of each the elements and how they complement one another. Wood complements fire by increasing its energy. Fire complements earth through its burning power which creates earth. Earth complements metal as metal is found in the earth. Metal takes on the quality of liquid (water) when heated. Water complements wood by nourishing it.

The cycle of conflicts exhibits the conflicts among the elements and how they can weaken one another. Wood conflicts with earth as it absorbs energy from earth. Fire conflicts with metal as it melts metal. Earth conflicts with water as it can absorb and pollute water. Metal conflicts with wood as metal breaks wood down in the form of an axe. Water conflicts with fire as it kills fire. However, these general applications are only relevant provided the elements are present on an equal basis. The weaker elements could overpower the stronger elements if they exceed the controlling power of the stronger element. For example, we would not be able to cut down an entire forest with a small axe despite the control metal has over wood. Similarly, with the cycle of complements, water may complement wood, but too much water would have a negative effect on wood. The right amount of water will nourish wood, but an excessive amount will damage wood.

Applying the principle of complements and conflicts is dependent on balancing the value of the five elements. In feng shui, this refers to the yin and yang qualities of each of the elements. Yin is the weaker (feminine) version of the elements and yang is the stronger (masculine) version of the elements. The yin and the yang must be balanced to maintain a harmonious living environment.

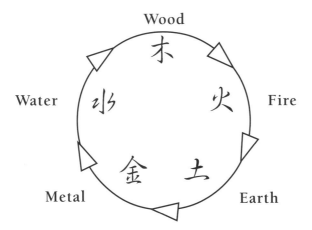

The cycle of complements of the five elements and their corresponding symbols.

A table of yin and yang qualities.

	Yin	Yang
Wood	Flowers & plants	Forest & jungles
Fire	Sparks & small fires	Large scale fire
Earth	Building materials	Mountains & valleys
Metal	Utensils & tools	Tin mines
Water	Streams & ponds	Oceans, rivers & waterfalls

The cycle of conflicts of the five elements.

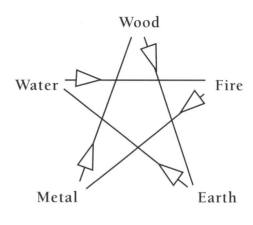

The five elements and their related colours, geometrical forms and directions.

Element	Colour	Form	Directions
Wood	Green	╱	East, Southeast
Fire	Red	▲	South
Earth	Yellow	■	Southwest, Northeast
Metal	White	●	West, Northwest
Water	Black	〜〜	North

Each of the five elements is associated with a colour, geometrical form and compass direction. The cycles of complements and conflicts also hold true for the colours and geometrical forms of the five elements. Green complements red, red complements yellow, yellow complements white and white complements black. Similarly, rectangles complement triangles, triangles complement squares, squares complement circles and circles complement irregular forms.

Understanding these associations will enable feng shui practitioners to incorporate the relevant elements into the home and workplace.

The colours and geometrical forms of the five elements in the cycle of complements.

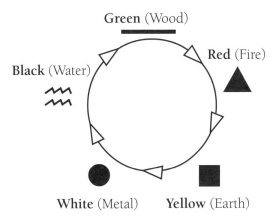

and 10 (earth) complement four and nine (metal). Four and nine (metal) complement one and six (water). One and six (water) complement three and eight (wood).

— — — ▶ *The Order of Complements*

East	South	Centre	West	North
Wood	Fire	Earth	Metal	Water
3, 8	2, 7	5, 10	4, 9	1, 6
Green	Red	Yellow	White	Black

Table 4.1 The He Tu applied to the five elements and their corresponding directions, numbers and colours in the cycle of complements.

The colours and geometrical forms of the five elements in the cycle of conflicts.

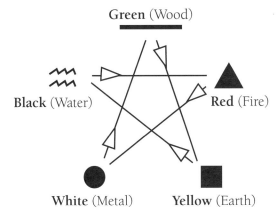

Similarly, the cycle of conflicts can be interpreted to mean that three and eight (wood) conflict with five and 10 (earth). Five and 10 (earth) conflict with one and six (water). One and six (water) conflict with two and seven (fire). Two and seven (fire) conflict with four and seven (metal). Four and nine (metal) conflict with three and eight (wood).

— — — ▶ *The Order of Conflicts*

East	Centre	North	South	West
Wood	Earth	Water	Fire	Metal
3, 8	5, 10	1, 6	2, 7	4, 9
Green	Yellow	Black	Red	White

Table 4.2 The He Tu applied to the five elements and their corresponding directions, numbers and colours in the cycle of conflicts.

The application of the cycles of complements and conflicts can be further enhanced when combined with the He Tu as mentioned earlier. Table 4.1 can be interpreted to mean that the numbers three and eight belong to the wood element and they complement the numbers two and seven which are of the fire element. Two and seven (fire) complement five and 10 (earth). Five

An individual's birth details can also be related to the five elements. Chinese astrology associates an animal to every year in a 12-year cycle. The five elements are also assigned in rotation to each year, making it a 60-year cycle (12 Chinese zodiac animals x five elements). Given these associations, the complements and conflicts among a person's year of birth, type of house, wall colours, shape of furniture and how they are placed become possible. In general, most feng shui practitioners work to balance the five elements within the given space of a room, the entire house, a city or even the country.

The Compass Directions and the Five Elements

The ancient Chinese geomancers had positioned south at the top of the compass, using China as the reference point. In the Chinese language, the word *China* literally means *Middle Kingdom* or *centre of the earth*.

In the history of geomancy, all fundamental systems and their basic theories were based on this understanding. The south with reference to the five elements represents fire and the north represents water. The east represents wood and the west represents metal. Earth, as represented by China, takes middle ground. These references were made according to geographical observations from the standpoint of China. It was believed that in the direction of the east, the strongest force was the wood element and in the west, metal. When combined with the Luo Shu, the characteristics and energies of the five elements and their corresponding directions, colours and geometrical symbols and numbers are greatly enhanced.

SE 4 Wood (Green)	▲ South 9 Fire (Red)	■ SW 2 Earth (Yellow)
East 3 Wood (Green)	■ Centre 5 Earth (Yellow)	● West 7 Metal (White)
■ NE 8 Earth (Yellow)	〰 North 1 Water (Black)	● NW 6 Metal (White)

The Luo numbers, directions and colours.

Applying the Five Elements

In accordance to traditional feng shui practices, certain three dimentional forms or altars in specific colours were used to deflect negative forces from the house. These items were usually positioned at the top of the front door or on top of windows, side gates or at the rear entrance. The items included brushes, talismans, wooden swords, flags and various designs of the ba gua. As most of these items were designed to suit the architecture of a particular period in history, some do not fit well into the modern context. Hence, these items have been modified with new forms and new designs.

The application of the principles of the five elements today comes in a combination of colours, forms and numerical references to the Heavenly numbers or He Tu. These principles are also used as a guideline for the number of objects to replace the actual five element colours or their forms. For example, when applying the fire element, the corresponding He Tu number to fire is two and seven. Wood in its five element principle complements fire. The numbers for wood are three and eight. Therefore, three and eight are complementary to the numbers two or seven, or to the south and to any element of fire. The different expressions of the five element principles for modern environments can be seen in the use of building materials such as glass blocks, plastic sheets and mirrors in the interior or exterior of buildings. For example, two or seven glass blocks would represent fire and would fit best into the southern side of the building. To further increase the fire force, triangular patterns may be painted around the blocks or the wall may even be painted red. This modern feng shui practice is known as the Hidden Force method.

Glass blocks made up of the numbers 1+8+1+4. 1, 4 and 8 represent prosperity and wealth.

The colours of the five elements are used in this building to generate energy. In modern colour schemes, blue is sometimes used to replace black. The green represents wood that fuels fire (red). Fire (red) generates earth (yellow) which creates metal (white) that is able to take on a liquified form (water), which is represented by the colour blue.

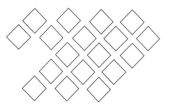

Diagram 1

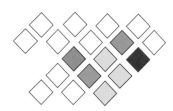

Diagram 2

Diagram 3

Diagram 4

Diagram 5

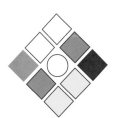

Diagram 6

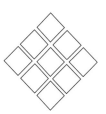

Diagram 7

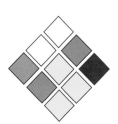

Diagram 8

Diagram 9

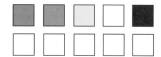

Diagram 10

These diagrams are examples of the Hidden Force method used today. The colour combinations and the number of blocks are representative of the ba gua. In diagrams 1 and 2, decorative blocks are placed around the main formation. The shapes of these decorative blocks may vary as desired. Diagram 10 is representative of the five elements in a complementary cycle from the left to the right. This arrangement may even be tilted at a 45° angle for visual impact.

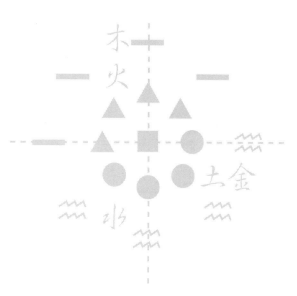

The Divine Creatures 四灵兽

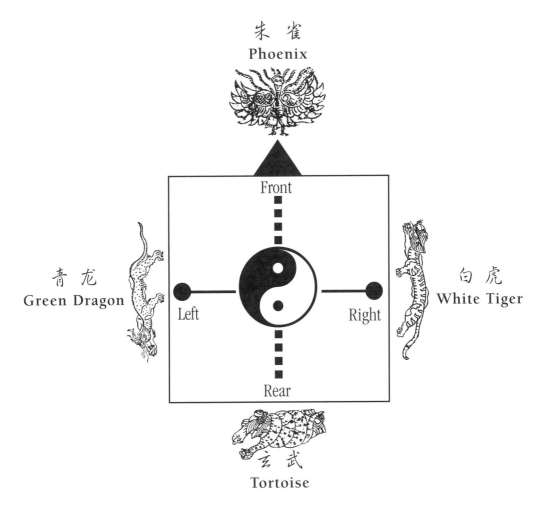

朱 雀
Phoenix

青龙
Green Dragon

Front

Left   Right

Rear

白虎
White Tiger

玄武
Tortoise

The four divine creatures came into feng shui applications by nature of their characteristics. It was believed that water flowing at the front of a house was auspicious. Thus, the phoenix, with its flapping wings, was believed to generate movement of the water elements, and was used to represent the front of a house.

High mountains at the back of a house was believed to offer protection and back support to the occupants. Thus, the tortoise was used to represent the back of the house. It was also known as the ruler of the north.

The west or yin sector was believed to be where inauspicious elements were located or hidden. The tiger, being firm and heavy would generate less movement and be able to keep these elements in check. It was thus used to represent the right side of the house and was also known as the ruler of the west.

The east or the yang sector was believed to be where the most positive forces were located and thus movement in this sector was auspicious. As such, the dragon, symbolic of roads with a constant flow of traffic, was used to represent the left side of the building. It was also known as the ruler of the east.

These principles were applied in the olden days when one could build a house anywhere, facing any direction one desired. However, these principles were gradually restricted when state guidelines for city designs were introduced. Despite the north, south, east and west directions that each of the creatures represented, they were generally also recognised as symbolising the front, the rear, the left and the right of a building. As such, the phoenix will always represent the front of the building, the tortoise always the rear, the dragon the left and the tiger the right, regardless of a building's facing.

The significance of the divine creatures continues to be a preferred guideline for dwellings today. Fountains are set at the front of buildings. The left side, where the green dragon is situated, is generally recommended for vehicle driveways which may be stretched all the way to the rear of the building to join the white tiger's path on the right. The right may be used as a heavy storage area.

In the interior, walkways or staircases are best set on the left and heavy furniture such as televisions and electronic systems are best located on the right. It may not, however, always be possible to adhere to the principles of the four divine creatures. As mentioned earlier in this book, there are many other feng shui applications and each method develops different effects of its own. One may thus choose to apply any of these other methods as is appropriate.

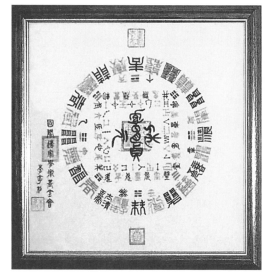

The circular tai chi talisman designed by Dr. Li Heng Lih covers all tai chi related information. It was designed in the spirit of Taoist philosophy and it is able to balance the magnetic forces in any environment.

These forces must be combined to make for effective feng shui.

Ego Force (50%)

+

Human Force (25%)

+

Environmental Force (25%)

Positive forces do not have the capacity to accommodate ill ego forces. Feng shui applications will not be effective with the presence of ill ego and bad human forces.

Good and Bad Feng Shui ...

The Expectations ...

Most people assume that feng shui has the power to perform wonders. They believe that applying the right methods would bring them wealth and prosperity. In my years of experience as a feng shui practitioner, I have come across many people with different expectations. The majority seek to change the feng shui of their homes in hope of greater wealth in the near future. Others, who have met with sudden illness or who believe that their homes are plagued with unhealthy qi, seek health. Still others hope to see a major improvement in their careers or their children's academic performance.

The attainment of wealth is a major preoccupation for many seekers of feng shui. But if by applying the principles of feng shui one could perform such miracles, all the feng shui practitioners would have turned themselves into very wealthy people by now. They would not need to work as feng shui practitioners anymore. Genuine feng shui practitioners, however, believe that they have been given a special understanding of the forces of nature and are able to help create a balanced and harmonious living and working environment for people, according to their individual magnetic fields. As such, feng shui practitioners do not attempt to enforce magnetic fields with the intention of achieving wealth beyond one's birth fields. An individual's magnetic field is set according to one's time and place of birth. The Chinese ancestors used these facts to observe and develop the metaphysical stages of the human being and from there, established the art of fate and geomancy.

In geomancy, it is believed that every object and place on earth possesses an individual and independent force. When one force comes into contact with another force, they create a magnetic field that changes the physical and psychological environment of the individual involved. Feng shui works to balance these aspects in order to enhance the individual's development and environment.

Combination of the Three Forces ...

While feng shui can help balance the magnetic forces in one's surroundings, it can only be made effective with the correct combination of the ego force, the human force and the environmental force. The three forces can be understood in this example.

When a person wants to achieve wealth (ego force), it will require a combined effort with the other two forces. To attain wealth, one has to work for it. This will also require working with other people (human force). One also has to be at a certain location such as the workplace (environmental force) in order to achieve this goal. It is the balance of these three forces that provides the ultimate force to fulfil the expectation.

In the practice of feng shui, the ego force plays a major role in determining whether an application is effective or not. This influence may increase if the person is able to adapt easily to the new environment and mix well with the people there. On the contrary, it can also decrease if a person is unable to fit into the new environment or mix around.

The ego force develops within the inner mind of the individual. A person who has wisdom, compassion and a cheerful deposition will develop positive forces and add energy to the ego force.

On the other hand, the ego force will automatically develop into a negative force if one harbours evil intentions, such as achieving wealth through unscrupulous means. The negative force will work against the other two forces and damage them. As a result of this imbalance, any gains achieved by the negative ego force will not be permanent. It might even reverse the circumstances of the individual and the people around him. For example, in the commercial sector, people who work to achieve wealth and status through unscrupulous means will also cause the people around him to lose their trust in one another, causing their working relationship to be strained. When the application of feng shui is abused or misused in any situation, the outcome will always be unpleasant.

The ego force is also generally developed through the religious inclinations of the individual. Religion develops the notion of fate within the inner mind and in most cases, this affects the effect of feng shui applications on a person who is so inclined. This may also hold true for free thinkers who may believe that they have the power within themselves to overcome all other forces. The application of feng shui becomes ineffective in this case.

Practical Feng Shui

**These are the
three main factors of
good environmental feng shui:**

Visibility

Accessibility

Amenity

**These are the
three main factors of
good household feng shui:**

Natural light

Air

Water

There are several feng shui methods that are practised today. As a result of different lifestyles, ethnic groups and religious backgrounds, the methods used by different feng shui practitioners may vary. The feng shui methods practised by those from the northern territory of China differs significantly from that of those who come from the south. Understandably, it also varies among those who come from different parts of the world.

The earliest methods passed down from northern China was mostly of the magnetic field method — the Compass School method. This method concentrates on the invisible directional magnetic forces. It is largely due to the wider open fields and the flatter geographical landscape of the north. In the south where the landscape is more hilly and there are more rivers cutting through the land, the methods applied are mostly based on the visibility of the landscape. This is known as the Form School.

Despite the different classifications, good feng shui is largely based on the visible formations in the surroundings, such as a location with pleasant views. A building with a stark object located directly at its front entrance is not considered to be auspicious.

Good environmental feng shui is assessed through the availability of the threefold qualities of visibility, accessibility and pleasant amenities. Modern feng shui practitioners have classified the factors of this assessment into three main elements. They are the visible, magnetic field and theological elements.

The Visible Element

In feng shui terminology, this is known as the Luan Tou method (峦头法). In essence, it refers to forms that are visible to the naked eye. This deals mainly with an individual's natural reaction towards an environment. It is the sense of ease or discomfort that a person feels upon his first encounter with a place. All factors and theories of feng shui become ineffective if a person does not feel at ease in an environment upon the first contact. Feng shui cannot be enforced in the hope that such an environment will be put right thereafter. It is important to locate a suitable environment in order to have good feng shui. This involves accessing a building's visible surroundings such as the directions in which the roads run and the rivers flow and how the trees grow. There should be a reasonable area of open space at the front of the building to allow a free flow of qi. At the back of the building, it would be ideal to have mountains or a group of big and tall buildings acting as a protective shield. Alternatively, a tall boundary rock wall would have the same effect. Within the building, sufficient sunlight, air flow and a good supply of water must also be available.

The Magnetic Field Elements

The magnetic field elements are also known as the Li Qi method (理气法), meaning *the principles of the force*. Once the visible elements of a location are achieved, the magnetic field elements in that particular environment may be studied. This deals mainly with the magnetic forces within or without a building, an office space or even a large housing estate. It even relates to an area as large as a country and its relationship with other countries.

The magnetic poles and the compass directions are the most crucial factors that impact our living environment, making the magnetic field elements the most complex of the three elements. An individual's magnetic force, calculated using one's birth details, is also required to assess one's relationship with the environment. The combination of the magnetic field elements and the visible elements of the environment will enable feng shui to be assessed and applied more effectively.

阳宅一错误三年
阴宅一错伤三代

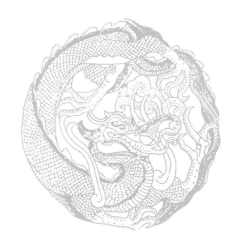

Any mistakes made in applying domestic feng shui will affect a person for three years, but any mistakes made in burial feng shui will affect three generations.

The Theological Elements

Also known as the Xuan Shen method (玄神法), the theological elements refer to an individual's spiritual beliefs. An individual's spiritual inclination can affect the outcome of feng shui applications as mentioned earlier.

The Xuan Shen method includes the use of wind chimes, talismans, mirrors, bamboo plants, ba gua and portraits of altars and other auspicious objects in a building or home. These objects are placed at selected points within the building to generate positive and negative fields to balance the forces in the environment. These forces work with the ego forces of the building's owner and the other occupants of the building. In this respect, it is vital to have the owner and occupants' faithful belief in the effectiveness of the feng shui applications. Doubts and suspicions concerning the feng shui consultant's advice will create negative forces and in most cases, it will affect the outcome of the feng shui effort. It is therefore vital for the owner of the building to ensure that all the other occupants also have full faith in the theological feng shui applications. The combined ego forces from all the participants will strengthen the power of the theological force which in turn, will maximise the effects of the feng shui applications carried out in the building.

The theological elements do not relate directly to religion. However, due to the religious background of most feng shui practitioners who may be Taoist or Buddhist, the methods that they apply will generally be referred to as a Buddhist or Taoist feng shui method. Feng shui was developed long before most of the religions of today. As such, the practise of feng shui should not be referred to as an extension of any religion.

The following pages highlight some of the theological feng shui settings and auspicious ornaments developed for the modern day environment.

The morning sun shines on feng shui ornaments in a home. These feng shui ornaments were designed by Dr. Li Heng Lih. They have the power to stabilise magnetic forces in a domestic environment.

Lu Dong Bin (吕洞宾) is one of the eight immortals in Chinese history. A picture of the immortal is believed to have the power to prevent evil sprits from entering a house.

The god of prosperity (财神) has the power to bring wealth to a home.

Fu Lu Shou (福禄寿) are the three deities who represent wealth, status and longivity. The bamboo plant and the picture of a robin represent happiness. This combination of items can be placed in both auspicious or inauspicious sectors of the house to generate good feng shui.

Guan Di (关帝) is the deity that has been recognised by both the Buddhist and Taoist as the god of protection. He gained his fame during the War of the Three Kingdoms. He is also known as the god of wealth.

Zhong Kui (锺馗) is the most popular ghost catcher in Chinese mythology. He has the power to immobilise negative forces and exorcise haunted houses. He is also known as the god of wealth and prosperity. This picture was designed by Dr. Li Heng Lih.

One of the most remarkable feng shui ornaments designed by Dr. Li Heng Lih is the wu chi tu (picture hanging in the background). It is the pictorial representation of the Nine Flying Stars and the tai chi. It has the power to stabilise environmental forces.

This talisman designed by Dr. Li Heng Lih is representative of all Chinese mythological talimans. It has the power to overcome any inauspicious forces indoors.

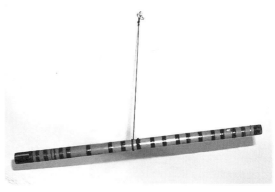

Hanging a sprig of spring onion, chive and celery together in the study room will help to increase a person's ability to concentrate while studying there. Do this on the third day of the second lunar month. This is the birthday of the god of literacy.
二月初三日，
文昌星君圣诞。

The flute or xiao (箫) has the same pronunciation as the word meaning dispel in Chinese. The flute is thus commonly placed at the inauspicious sectors of a house to dispel bad luck.

Burning incense can dissolve stagnant magnetic forces in the house. It will also help to balance the ego force of the individual.

Chapter 5
The Auspicious Sectors

*I*n seeking out the auspicious and inauspicious sectors of any given space, most feng shui practitioners use the Ba Zhai method (八宅法). This is also known as the Eight Territorial method. Under this methodology, the space is divided into eight sectors according to compass directions. This principle can be applied to a room, a house, an office block or even an entire city.

The ancients used this principle to divide land into eight sectors. A ninth sector was included to represent the middle palace (中宫). These sectors were grouped into a 3x3 square grid and known as the Nine Palace.

The Nine Palace was the fundamental structure for Oriental space usage. It was also used to locate the auspicious and inauspicious sectors within any given space. It is believed

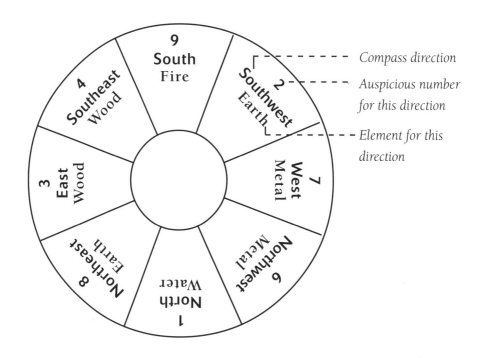

Compass direction

Auspicious number for this direction

Element for this direction

Southeast Xun (Wood)	**South** Li (Fire)	**Southwest** - - - *Compass direction* Kun - - - - - *Corresponding gua* (Earth) *(or Eight Trigram) for* *this direction*
East Zhen (Wood)	**Centre** (Earth)	**West** - - - - - *Corresponding element for* Dui *this direction* (Metal)
Northeast Gen (Earth)	**North** Kan (Water)	**Northwest** Qian (Metal)

The Nine Palace. Each palace (square) is associated with one of the five elements and a gua. The centre palace is known as the middle palace.

that a square-shaped piece of land was the most auspicious for building purposes. It was the fundamental requirement for good feng shui. The next best was a circular land area.

Triangular and odd-shaped lands should be avoided as these shapes tend to generate uneven magnetic fields, making it hard to achieve good feng shui.

The Feng Shui Compass

To locate the auspicious zones within a house or a building, a compass is first used to determine the facing of the structure. The compass that feng shui practitioners use is known as the luo pan. The name luo pan translates to mean *a table that consists of all universal information.*

The luo pan used by different clans of practitioners varies and some have more rings of information than others. However, not all sections within a luo pan are applicable for dividing houses and buildings. Some of these

sections were designed to measure the position of burial grounds and some of them for locating the directions of other magnetic fields. Today, most feng shui practitioners will only use the luo pan to locate the seating and facing direction of a building.

For greater accuracy in determining the facing direction of a building, both the luo pan and a traveller's compass must be used. Care must also be taken to ensure that the readings are not affected by household appliances or any items with a magnetic field.

A luo pan, the geomancer's compass.

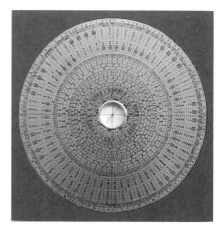

Different types of luo pan.

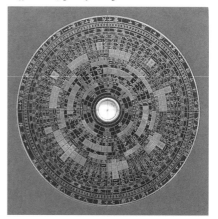

A traveller's compass.

The compass at the Forbidden City, Beijing, China.

When the direction of a house is in between readings, for example, its general facing direction is southwest, but it is inclined more towards the west, the house is considered a western clan house. Buildings can be classified into either the western clan or the eastern clan.

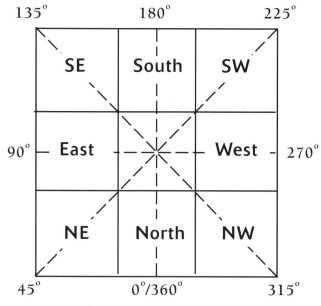

The standard directions and the corresponding degrees.

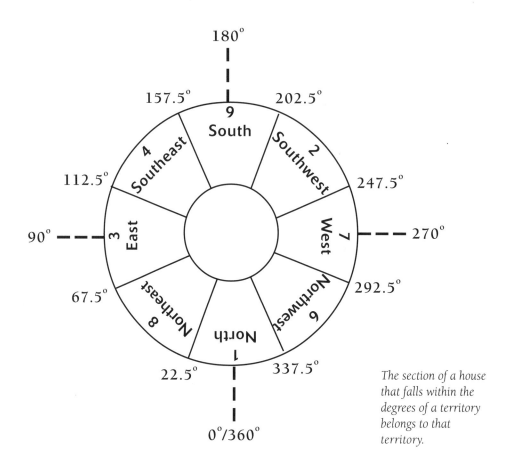

The section of a house that falls within the degrees of a territory belongs to that territory.

The Nine Palaces

The Nine Palace grid originated from the Ba Zhai. It was put into a square format for easy reference. However, when assessing the floor plan of a building, it would be more accurate to use the Ba Zhai grid as it is easier to do an imaginary extension of the lines demarcating the different directions. This would enable one to cover a wider area when reading the floor plans.

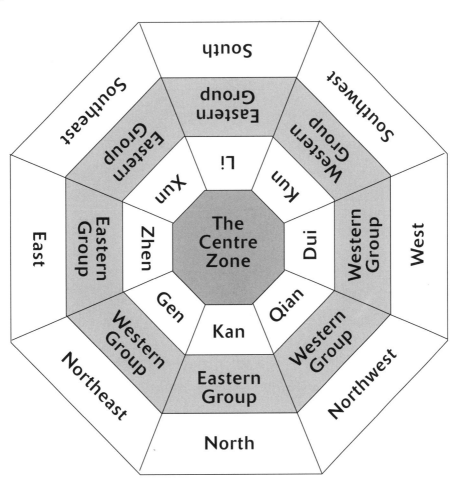

The Ba Zhai directions and clan groups.

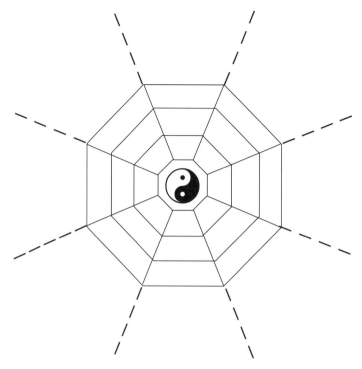

Each section can be easily extended to cover a wider area.

SE Eastern Group **Xun**	South Eastern Group **Li**	SW Western Group **Kun**
East Eastern Group **Zhen**	**The Centre Zone**	West Western Group **Dui**
NE Western Group **Gen**	North Eastern Group **Kan**	NW Western Group **Qian**

— — — — *Compass direction*

— — — *Life group*

— — — *Gua*

The Eastern and the Western Clans

The sections within the Nine Palace grid are classified into two main clans known as the eastern clan and the western clan ...

Each clan occupies four auspicious sectors and four inauspicious sectors. The four auspicious sectors of the western clan are west, southwest, northwest and northeast and the four auspicious sectors of the eastern clan are north, south, east and southeast. The auspicious sectors of the western clan are the inauspicious sectors of the eastern clan and vice versa. It is within these sectors that feng shui practitioners apply the principles of positive and negative forces.

Both male and female are also classified into two major groups known as the eastern life group and the western life group.

Each again comprises four auspicious life groups and four inauspicious life groups. The centre section may be either auspicious or inauspicious for each group. This will depend on whether the clan and life group of a person matches. A person belonging to the eastern life group and living in any of the eastern clan sectors will have an additional auspicious sector — the centre zone.

Similarly, a person belonging to the western life group should ideally live within the western clan sectors in order to achieve an additional auspicious sector. When a person's life group does not correspond with the clan sector, the person will have four auspicious sectors and five inauspicious sectors in his home. The centre section becomes inauspicious for the person.

The classification of an individual into either the eastern or western life group is based on the individual's year of birth. Both the eastern and western life groups are based on the yin and the yang principles. The eastern clan is referred to as the yang sector. It is the direction in which the sun rises. The western clan is referred to as the yin sector. This is the direction in which the sun sets. There is no northern life or southern life within these principles. The north and south are the top and bottom of the earth.

The individual life group classifications are applied to establish the location for an individual's good fate and fortune. For example, a person who belongs to the eastern life group would find his health and fortune in the north, south, east or southeastern areas of the country in which he resides. The person who belongs to the western life group will on the other hand find his health and fortune in the west, southwest, northwest and northeast areas of the country. This principle is also applied indoors, in the home or office.

The auspicious sectors would be the ideal areas for the person to sleep or work in. In most cases, feng shui practitioners will apply the principles of the five elements within the auspicious sectors to increase the magnetic force and at the same time reduce the negative magnetic energy of the inauspicious sectors. For example, if the south is an auspicious sector for a person, the wood element is increased to add strength to the fire element of the south (wood fuels fire).

The table shows the main feng shui life group for those born between 1933 and 2010. The year of birth is based on the lunar calendar. For those born between the last week of January and the second week of February, their life group might be different from what is shown below.

	Male	Female		Male	Female		Male	Female
1933	Eastern	Western	1959	Western	Eastern	1985	Western	Eastern
1934	Eastern	Eastern	1960	Eastern	Western	1986	Western	Eastern
1935	Western	Eastern	1961	Eastern	Eastern	1987	Eastern	Western
1936	Eastern	Western	1962	Western	Eastern	1988	Eastern	Eastern
1937	Eastern	Western	1963	Eastern	Western	1989	Western	Eastern
1938	Western	Western	1964	Eastern	Western	1990	Eastern	Western
1939	Western	Western	1965	Western	Western	1991	Eastern	Western
1940	Western	Eastern	1966	Western	Western	1992	Western	Western
1941	Western	Eastern	1967	Western	Eastern	1993	Western	Western
1942	Eastern	Western	1968	Western	Eastern	1994	Western	Eastern
1943	Eastern	Eastern	1969	Eastern	Western	1995	Western	Eastern
1944	Western	Eastern	1970	Eastern	Eastern	1996	Eastern	Western
1945	Eastern	Western	1971	Western	Eastern	1997	Eastern	Eastern
1946	Eastern	Western	1972	Eastern	Western	1998	Western	Eastern
1947	Western	Western	1973	Eastern	Western	1999	Eastern	Western
1948	Western	Western	1974	Western	Western	2000	Eastern	Western
1949	Western	Eastern	1975	Western	Western	2001	Western	Western
1950	Western	Eastern	1976	Western	Eastern	2002	Western	Western
1951	Eastern	Western	1977	Western	Eastern	2003	Western	Eastern
1952	Eastern	Eastern	1978	Eastern	Western	2004	Western	Eastern
1953	Western	Eastern	1979	Eastern	Eastern	2005	Eastern	Western
1954	Eastern	Western	1980	Western	Eastern	2006	Eastern	Eastern
1955	Eastern	Western	1981	Eastern	Western	2007	Western	Eastern
1956	Western	Western	1982	Eastern	Western	2008	Eastern	Western
1957	Western	Western	1983	Western	Western	2009	Eastern	Western
1958	Western	Eastern	1984	Western	Western	2010	Western	Western

The auspicious sectors of the eastern clans.

4 Wood SE	9 Fire South	/////
3 Wood East	The classification of the centre zone depends on one's life group	/////
/////	1 Water North	/////

The auspicious sectors of the western clans.

/////	/////	2 Earth SW
/////	The classification of the centre zone depends on one's life group	7 Metal West
8 Earth NE	/////	6 Metal NW

Clan Groups and the Ba Gua

The feng shui clan groups can be divided into four different levels of auspiciousness. This is related to the Earthly ba gua. Each of the four clan groups from the eastern and western groups belong to a gua in the Earthly ba gua.

There are four positive guas and four negative guas in the Earthly ba gua. The positive guas are Qian (乾), Kan (坎), Gen (艮) and Zhen (震). These are the four yang gua (四阳卦). The negative guas are known as the four yin gua (四阴卦). They are Xun (巽), Li (离), Kun (坤) and Dui (兑).

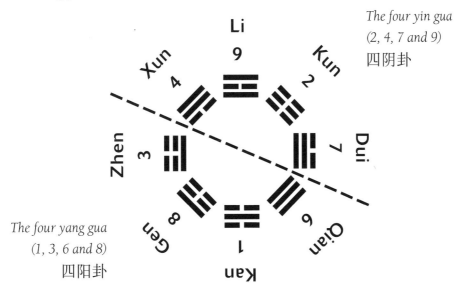

The four yin gua (2, 4, 7 and 9)
四阴卦

The four yang gua (1, 3, 6 and 8)
四阳卦

Life groups and their ba gua relations.

	Male	Female		Male	Female		Male	Female
1933	Xun (E)	Kun (W)	1959	Kun (W)	Kan (E)	1995	Qian (W)	Li (E)
1934	Zhen (E)	Zhen (E)	1960	Xun (E)	Kun (W)	1986	Kun (W)	Kan (E)
1935	Kun (W)	Xun (E)	1961	Zhen (E)	Zhen (E)	1987	Xun (E)	Kun (W)
1936	Kan (E)	Gen (W)	1962	Kun (W)	Xun (E)	1988	Zhen (E)	Zhen (E)
1937	Li (E)	Qian (W)	1963	Kan (E)	Gen (W)	1989	Kun (W)	Xun (E)
1938	Gen (W)	Dui (W)	1964	Li (E)	Qian (W)	1990	Kan (E)	Gen (W)
1939	Dui (W)	Gen (W)	1965	Gen (W)	Dui (W)	1991	Li (E)	Qian (W)
1940	Qian (W)	Li (E)	1966	Dui (W)	Gen (W)	1992	Gen (W)	Dui (W)
1941	Kun (W)	Kan (E)	1967	Qian (W)	Li (E)	1993	Dui (W)	Gen (W)
1942	Xun (E)	Kun (W)	1968	Kun (W)	Kan(E)	1994	Qian (W)	Li (E)
1943	Zhen (E)	Zhen (E)	1969	Xun (E)	Kun (W)	1995	Kun (W)	Kan (E)
1944	Kun (W)	Xun (E)	1970	Zhen (E)	Zhen (E)	1996	Xun (E)	Kun (W)
1945	Kan (E)	Gen (W)	1971	Kun (W)	Xun (E)	1997	Zhen (E)	Zhen (E)
1946	Li (E)	Qian (W)	1972	Kan (E)	Gen (W)	1998	Kun (W)	Xun (E)
1947	Gen (W)	Dui (W)	1973	Li (E)	Qian (W)	1999	Kan (E)	Gen (W)
1948	Dui (W)	Gen (W)	1974	Gen (W)	Dui (W)	2000	Li (E)	Qian (W)
1949	Qian (W)	Li (E)	1975	Dui (W)	Gen (W)	2001	Gen (W)	Dui (W)
1950	Kun (W)	Kan (E)	1976	Qian (W)	Li (E)	2002	Dui (W)	Gen (W)
1951	Xun (E)	Kun (W)	1977	Kun (W)	Kan (E)	2003	Qian (W)	Li (E)
1952	Zhen (E)	Zhen (E)	1978	Xun (E)	Kun (W)	2004	Kun (W)	Kan (E)
1953	Kun (W)	Xun (E)	1979	Zhen (E)	Zhen (E)	2005	Xun (E)	Kun (W)
1954	Kan (E)	Gen (W)	1980	Kun (W)	Xun (E)	2006	Zhen (E)	Zhen (E)
1955	Li (E)	Qian (W)	1981	Kan (E)	Gen (W)	2007	Kun (W)	Xun (E)
1956	Gen (W)	Dui (W)	1982	Li (E)	Qian (W)	2008	Kan (E)	Gen (W)
1957	Dui (W)	Gen (W)	1983	Gen (W)	Dui (W)	2009	Li (E)	Qian (W)
1958	Qian (W)	Li (E)	1984	Dui (W)	Gen (W)	2010	Gen (W)	Dui (W)

Note: Letters in brackets indicate eastern (E) life or western (W) life groups.

Each gua is associated with either a eastern life group or a western life group. In this association, they are neither positive nor negative. The four eastern life gua are north, Kan (坎), south, Li (离), east, Zhen (震) and southeast, Xun (巽). The four western life gua are northeast, Qian (乾), southeast, Kun (坤), east, Dui (兑) and northeast, Gen (艮).

Each gua is also associated with a compass direction and a zone (or qi). These zones have individual characteristics which indicate the different levels of auspiciousness in each direction. The four auspicious zones are Sheng Qi (生气), Tian Yi (天医), Yan Nian (延年) and Fu Wei (伏位). The four inauspicious zones are Jue Ming (绝命), Wu Gui (五鬼), Huo Hai (祸害) and Liu Sha (六煞).

The zones have no fixed position. They vary according to the life group of a person and the facing direction of the building being assessed. The auspiciousness of each zone is as follows:

Rank and properties of the four auspicious zones (四吉方).

Auspicious Zones		Rank	Properties
Sheng Qi	生气	Best	Prosperity and wealth
Tian Yi	天医	↓	Harmony and health
Yan Nian	延年		Longevity and happiness
Fu Wei	伏位	Good	Peace and stability

Rank and properties of the four inauspicious zones (四凶方).

Inauspicious Zones		Rank	Properties
Jue Ming	绝命	Bad	Poor wealth and disaster
Wu Gui	五鬼	↓	Disruption and theft
Huo Hai	祸害		Ill fate and sickness
Liu Sha	六煞	Worst	Unrest and failure

It is from these references and a person's year of birth that a geomancer is able to determine the best use of each room and the ideal location of household furnishings and other items.

Eastern Life Groups and the Directions

1. Refer to page 74 for your life group.
2. Refer to page 76 for your ba zhai group.
3. Refer to the following tables if you belong to the eastern life group.

Eastern Life Group — Auspicious Directions

	Sheng Qi 1 ✔ (Best)	Tian Yi 2 ✔	Yan Nian 3 ✔	Fu Wei 4 ✔ (Good)
Kan Life	Southeast	East	South	North
Li Life	East	Southeast	North	South
Zhen Life	South	North	Southeast	East
Xun Life	North	South	East	Southeast

Eastern Life Group — Inauspicious Directions

	Jue-Ming 1 ✘ (Bad)	Wu-Gui 2 ✘	Huo-Hai 3 ✘	Liu-Sha 4 ✘ (Worst)
Kan Life	Southwest	Northeast	West	Northwest
Li Life	Northwest	West	Northeast	Southwest
Zhen Life	West	Northwest	Southwest	Northeast
Xun Life	Northeast	Southwest	Northwest	West

Western Life Groups and the Directions

1. Refer to page 74 for your life group.
2. Refer to page 76 for your ba zhai group.
3. Refer to the following tables if you belong to the western life group.

Western Life Group — Auspicious Directions

	Sheng Qi 1 ✔ (Best)	Tian Yi 2 ✔	Yan Nian 3 ✔	Fu Wei 4 ✔ (Good)
Qian Life	West	Northeast	Southwest	Northwest
Kun Life	Northeast	West	Northwest	Southwest
Gen Life	Southwest	Northwest	West	Northeast
Dui Life	Northwest	Southwest	West	Northeast

Western Life Group — Inauspicious Directions

	Jue Ming 1 ✘ (Bad)	Wu Gui 2 ✘	Huo Hai 3 ✘	Liu Sha 4 ✘ (Worst)
Qian Life	South	East	Southeast	North
Kun Life	Norh	Southeast	East	South
Gen Life	Southeast	North	South	East
Dui Life	East	South	North	Southeast

Sectors of the Eastern Clan Groups

These are the auspicious directions for those buildings belonging to the eastern clan group. These are also the inauspicious directions for those in the western clan group.

SE	South	
East	☯	
	North	

1✔ SE	3✔ South	1✘ SW
2✔ East	**Kan**	3✘ West
2✘ NE	4✔ North	4✘ NW

2✔ SE	4✔ South	4✘ SW
1✔ East	**Li**	2✘ West
3✘ NE	3✔ North	1✘ NW

3✔ SE	1✔ South	3✘ SW
4✔ East	**Zhen**	1✘ West
4✘ NE	2✔ North	2✘ NW

4✔ SE	2✔ South	2✘ SW
3✔ East	**Xun**	4✘ West
1✘ NE	1✔ North	3✘ NW

Sectors of the Western Clan Groups

These are the auspicious directions for those buildings belonging to the western clan group. These are also the inauspicious directions for those in the eastern clan group.

		SW
	☯	West
NE		NW

3✗ SE	1✗ South	3✔ SW		2✗ SE	4✗ South	4✔ SW
2✗ East	**Qian**	1✔ West		3✗ East	**Kun**	2✔ West
2✔ NE	4✗ North	4✔ NW		1✔ NE	1✗ North	3✔ NW

1✗ SE	3✗ South	1✔ SW		4✗ SE	2✗ South	2✔ SW
4✗ East	**Gen**	3✔ West		1✗ East	**Dui**	4✔ West
4✔ NE	2✗ North	2✔ NW		3✔ NE	3✗ North	1✔ NW

Auspicious and Inauspicious Sectors

The auspicious sectors are best used as bedrooms, study rooms and sitting rooms. Beds and tables may be placed in the inner auspicious sections in each sector while trash bins, stoves, refrigerators and laundry baskets may be put in the inner inauspicious sections. The inauspicious sectors within a house are best used to locate toilets, storerooms and guestrooms. In the situation when auspicious sectors are unsuitable for placing furniture and other fixtures because of the presence of a door, a window or a built-in cupboard, the next best location will have to be used instead. As not all houses will suit every owner's life group, it is wise to first locate the auspicious direction that matches one's life group and bear that in mind when purchasing property.

4 Wood SE	9 Fire South	
3 Wood East	The classification of the centre zone depends on one's life group	
	1 Water North	

The eastern life group's auspicious sectors.

The eastern life group's inner auspicious sectors.

For those belonging to the eastern life group, the southeast, east, south and north are auspicious sectors. These sectors are suitable for the location of the main gate, main door, bedroom, study room and sitting room.

SE	South	////////
East	Centre zone is auspicious	////////
////////	North	////////

The eastern life group's auspicious sectors.

The shaded areas are the inauspicious sectors. They are suitable for the location of the garage, kitchen, toilet and storeroom.

The shaded areas are the inauspicious sectors. They are suitable for the location of the garage, kitchen, toilet and storeroom.

////////	////////	South west
////////	Centre zone is auspicious	West
North east	////////	North west

The western life group's auspicious sectors.

For those belonging to the western life group, the southwest, west, northwest and northeast are the auspicious sectors. These sectors are suitable for the location of the main gate, main door, bedroom, study room and sitting room.

Find your auspicious sectors.

The details below are for a man born in 1962, living in a western clan house.

Year of birth: **July 1962**	Male/Female : **Male**
Life group clan : (page 74) **Western Group**	Personal gua group : (page 76) **Kun**
House clan group : (page 81) **Western Clan**	House gua group : (page 71) **Qian**

Auspicious sectors :   *(If one's life group and house clan both belong to the same clan, the centre section is also auspicious. page 79)*

West, Southwest, Northwest, Northeast, Centre.

Life group's element :   *(If one's life group is Kun, the corresponding element is Earth, page 67)*

Earth

House group's element :   *(Assuming this house is seated northwest and faces southeast, the house is a Qian house. Qian's corresponding element is Metal (page 67).*

Metal

The Auspicious Sectors: *(To locate the auspicious and inauspicious sectors for a Qian house, refer to the table for Qian (page 81).)*	1✔ (Best) West	2✔ NE	3✔ SW	4✔ (Good) NW
The Inauspicious Sectors:	1✘ (Bad) South	2✘ East	3✘ SE	4✘ (Worst) North

Use the form below to fill in your details.

Your year of birth:	Male/Female :
Your life group clan :	Your gua group :
Your house clan group :	Your house gua group :
Your auspicious sectors :	
Your life group's element :	
Your house group's element :	

Your auspicious sectors: *(To locate the auspicious and inauspicious sectors for a Qian house, refer to the tables on pages 78 and 79.)*	1✔ (Best)	2✔	3✔	4✔ (Good)
Your Inauspicious sectors:	1✘ (Bad)	2✘	3✘	4✘ (Worst)

Judging Domestic Feng Shui from a Floor Plan

In order to identify the individual sectors of a house, its direction must first be determined. Set a reliable compass in the centre point of the area to check the seating and facing directions of the house. The centre point of the house is determined by drawing two diagonal lines across the floor plan.

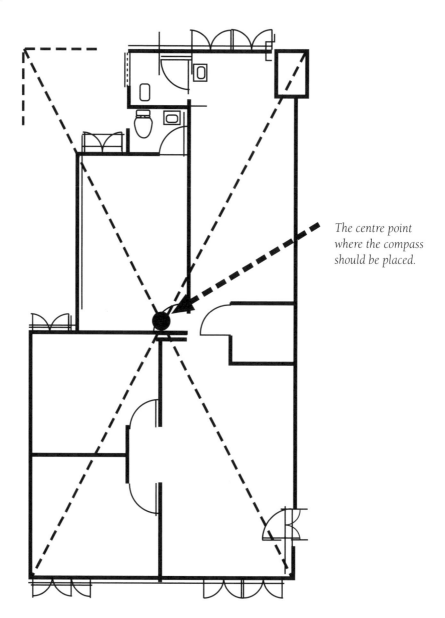

The centre point where the compass should be placed.

Assuming that an apartment is positioned 320° northwest and faces southeast at 140°, the apartment belongs to the western clan group. Its gua group is Qian. This is known as a Qian apartment. Its element is Metal (refer page 67). This apartment is suitable for those who belong to the western life group.

Northwest *(Metal)*
320°

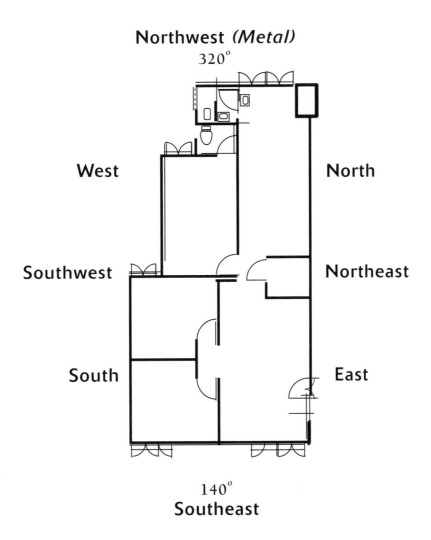

West

North

Southwest

Northeast

South

East

140°
Southeast

The auspicious sectors in this apartment are northeast, west, southwest and northwest. The floor plan shows that there are some sections missing in the west and northwest sections (top left hand corner). As these areas are in the auspicious sectors, it means that the apartment has fewer auspicious areas. In addition to this, the toilet is also located in an auspicious sector. As such, the apartment requires the application of more feng shui elements to make up for these losses.

Assuming that the owner of the apartment belongs to the western life group which matches that of the apartment, the centre zone would be considered auspicious as well. In this apartment, the centre auspicious zone is the meeting point of the doors and the room partitions. The door of the master bedroom and the entrance to the kitchen are located in this zone. They are thus considered to be auspicious doorways.

The other auspicious zones are the main entrance and the hall. Although they are located in the inauspicious east sectors, they face the auspicious northeast direction where the sun enters the hall from the door in the morning, transforming them into an auspicious zone. They are thus situated in the best zone of the apartment.

The kitchen is located across two sectors with the left in the auspicious sector and the right in the inauspicious sector. It is therefore important to place the stove or garbage bin within the inauspicious sector.

Qian (Western Group)

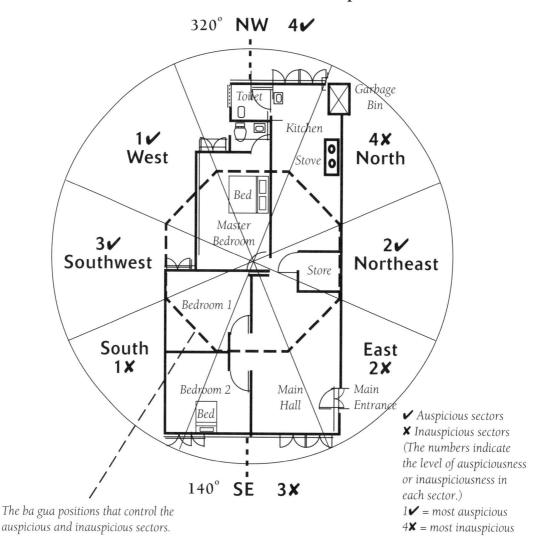

The ba gua positions that control the auspicious and inauspicious sectors.

✔ *Auspicious sectors*
✘ *Inauspicious sectors*
(The numbers indicate the level of auspiciousness or inauspiciousness in each sector.)
1✔ *= most auspicious*
4✘ *= most inauspicious*

The less ideal aspects of this apartment are that two of the bedrooms are situated in inauspicious sectors while the toilet is in an auspicious sector. In this situation, the beds in the bedrooms should be placed in the auspicious sector of the occupant's personal life group instead. Bedroom 1 is located in an inauspicious sector and may be used as a guestroom. The merit of this layout, however, is that most of the bedroom doors are located within the auspicious centre sector. While it is hard to obtain an ideal apartment that matches all our criteria, effort can be made to achieve the best use for the various rooms. The feng shui conditions of the apartment shown in the example are considered acceptable as the beds can be placed at the individual occupant's auspicious sectors and most of the doors are all in the auspicious zones. Apart from the location of the toilet...

...this apartment can be considered to be a good feng shui apartment.

Direction	Five Element	Colour	Form	Heavenly Numbers	Luo Numbers
North	Water	Black	〰〰	1, 6	1
South	Fire	Red	▲	2, 7	9
East	Wood	Green	▬	3, 8	3
West	Metal	White	●	4, 9	7
Northeast	Earth	Yellow	■	5, 10	8
Southeast	Wood	Green	▬	3, 8	4
Northwest	Metal	White	●	4, 9	6
Southwest	Earth	Yellow	■	5, 10	2
Centre	Earth	Yellow	■	5, 10	5

Using Colour to Strengthen the Sectors

Each of the Nine Palaces corresponds to a colour and a geometrical form related to the five elements. The principle of the five elements can be applied to strengthen the forces within the auspicious sectors and weaken that of the inauspicious sectors. This is done by applying the principle of the cycle of complements and conflicts.

In this instance, the feng shui for the whole building could be improved if the application of colour and geometrical forms is correct. The diagram below shows the colours and the geometrical forms associated with each of the sectors. This is regardless of the direction of the building. South will aways belong to the fire element. Red is its colour and the triangle is its geometrical form. Likewise, northwest will aways belong to the metal element. White is its colour and its geometrical form is a circle.

▬ **SE 4** (Green) Wood	▲ **South 9** (Red) Fire	■ **SW 2** (Yellow) Earth
▬ **East 3** (Green) Wood	■ **Centre 5** (Yellow) Earth	● **West 7** (White) Metal
■ **NE 8** (Yellow) Earth	〰 **North 1** (Black) Water	● **NW 6** (White) Metal

The Luo numbers, colours and geometrical forms associated with each sector.

Weakening the Forces in an Inauspicious Sector

Let's take the inauspicious east sector as an example. Its element is wood. In this case, the elements within the sector must be weakened in order to reduce its negative qi. This can be achieved by adding the fire element as fire will draw energy from wood and weaken it. Fire elements which may be used include items such as red carpets, red bed covers and red paint for the walls. The fire element can be further strengthened by using the element's heavenly numbers, two or seven. This could be represented with two or seven chairs or a picture of two or seven triangles (the triangle is the geometrical form for fire). The floor plan of the apartment shows that the south sector is a bedroom. Practically, it is not ideal to place seven chairs in a bedroom, but hanging a picture of two or seven chairs is fine. Feng shui applications must be functional to ensure that the application serves its purpose.

The auspicious west and northwest sectors (metal element), can be strengthened by adding the complementary colour (yellow) and geometrical form (square) of earth, since earth gives rise to metal. Conflicting elements such as water and fire must not be used. Fire will melt metal and water will weaken metal by absorbing its properties. In these sectors, red (fire) and black (water) are not suitable. Similarly, triangular (fire) and irregular (water) forms are also not suitable.

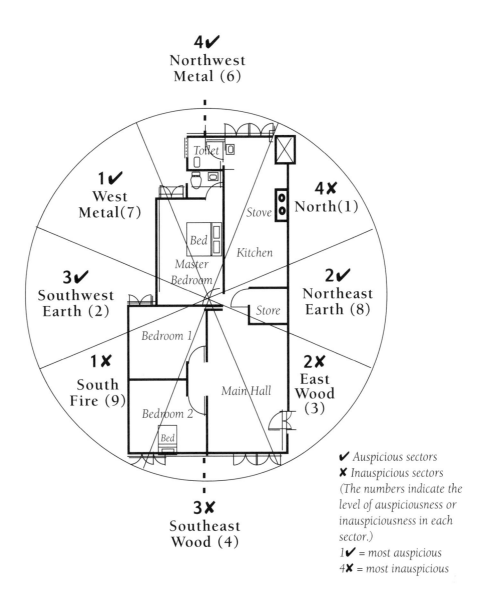

4✔
Northwest
Metal (6)

1✔
West
Metal(7)

4✘
North(1)

Toilet

Stove

Bed

Master Bedroom

Kitchen

3✔
Southwest
Earth (2)

Store

2✔
Northeast
Earth (8)

Bedroom 1

1✘
South
Fire (9)

Main Hall

2✘
East
Wood
(3)

Bedroom 2

Bed

3✘
Southeast
Wood (4)

✔ *Auspicious sectors*
✘ *Inauspicious sectors*
(The numbers indicate the level of auspiciousness or inauspiciousness in each sector.)
1✔ = most auspicious
4✘ = most inauspicious

Life Group Different from the House Group

Let us now assume that the same apartment (western group) is used by someone who belongs to the eastern life group. The difference in the life group and the house group would mean that the centre of the apartment is now an inauspicious sector. The other auspicious and inauspicious sectors of the apartment, however, remain the same since the sectors were calculated using the house group. The new owner would use these sectors in a way similar to the western life group person, except that he cannot use the centre of the apartment as it is an inauspicious sector for him. He should also place his bed where it used to be an inauspicious sector as it is now his life group's auspicious sector.

When one's life group is different from one's house group, the use of space becomes limited. Strengthening or weakening the forces using colour, geometrical forms or the heavenly numbers becomes more critical. It is also a more delicate procedure. Weakening the inauspicious sectors in the house would at the same time weaken the homeowner's individual life group sector.

Due to the resulting complications when a house group does not match with one's life group, it is advisable to find an apartment where the groups match. Matching groups would generally increase the entire force strength within the apartment and improve the fate of the homeowner.

... The feng shui of the apartment becomes complicated when the clan groups do not match ...

In a standard household, the occupants generally belong to different life groups. In this case, only the life group of the registered owner of the house is used to judge the auspicious and inauspicious sectors. The fate of the other occupants of the house would be based on the fate of the owner.

In the case of rented property, the life group of the lead tenant is used instead of the landlord's. Similarly, in an office, the life group of the boss is used. There will be complications when the company is a partnership. In this case, the life group of the partner who stays in the office and deals with internal matters is used. The other partners who deal with external matters and are not in the office much need not be considered. There are cases, however, where all the partners work in different offices within the same premises. Here, the life groups need not be considered. Instead, it is enough to ensure that the partners' offices are situated in the auspicious sectors of the building. The element corresponding to the year of birth of each partner must be referred to in order to match it with the sector's element. The two elements should be complementary.

The table shows the five elements corresponding to each year from 1933 to 2010, based on the lunar calendar. This table, however, should only be used as an additional reference to the clan and life groups methods.

Year of Birth	Element	Year of Birth	Element	Year of Birth	Element
1933	Metal	1959	Wood	1985	Metal
1934	Fire	1960	Earth	1986	Fire
1935	Fire	1961	Earth	1987	Fire
1936	Water	1962	Metal	1988	Wood
1937	Water	1963	Metal	1989	Wood
1938	Earth	1964	Fire	1990	Earth
1939	Earth	1965	Fire	1991	Earth
1940	Metal	1966	Water	1992	Metal
1941	Metal	1967	Water	1993	Metal
1942	Wood	1968	Earth	1994	Fire
1943	Wood	1969	Earth	1995	Fire
1944	water	1970	Metal	1996	Water
1945	Water	1971	Metal	1997	Water
1946	Earth	1972	Wood	1998	Earth
1947	Earth	1973	Wood	1999	Earth
1948	Fire	1974	Water	2000	Metal
1949	Fire	1975	Water	2001	Metal
1950	Wood	1976	Earth	2002	Wood
1951	Wood	1977	Earth	2003	Wood
1952	Water	1978	Fire	2004	Water
1953	Water	1979	Fire	2005	Water
1954	Metal	1980	Wood	2006	Earth
1955	Metal	1981	Wood	2007	Earth
1956	Fire	1982	Water	2008	Fire
1957	Fire	1983	Water	2009	Fire
1958	Wood	1984	Metal	2010	Wood

五行纳音

The Chinese almanac calendar of birth signs.

Chapter 6

Feng Shui and the Interior Part 1

The Directions

Under the principles of feng shui, the main door of an apartment may not necessarily indicate the facing direction of a building. The facing direction has to be determined from the position of the entire block. This is determined by the location of the main road leading to the building's main entrance.

While most buildings are designed with a distinctive difference between the front and the back, there are buildings where the front and the back are not easily distinguished. Examples of such buildings are point-block apartments where several units occupy the same floor and each unit faces a different

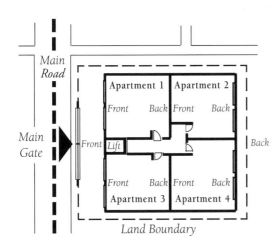

The facing direction of a point-block apartment is determined by the location of the main road.

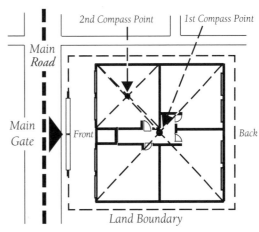

Setting the compass for a regularly shaped point-block apartment with four units on each floor.

direction. In this case, the section of the building that faces the main road would be judged as the front. The back would be the seating position of the building. A compass will have to be set at the centre point of the building to determine the facing and seating directions. The direction of the individual units would then follow the direction of the main building regardless of the position of the front doors of each unit. The compass may then be set at the centre of the unit to locate the auspicious and inauspicious sectors within the apartment. In the case of extended blocks where the units are connected by common corridors or staircases, both the left and the right wings are considered to be a single building. Locating the auspicious and inauspicious sectors is done by setting the compass at the centre point of the entire block. The individual units are then assessed accordingly.

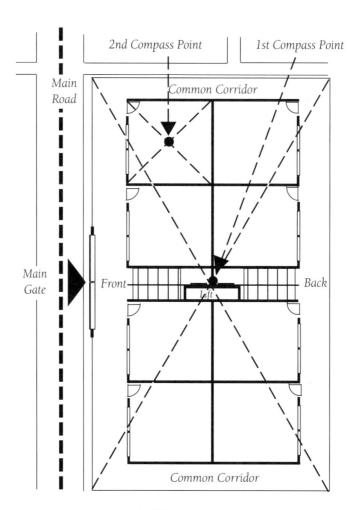

An extended block with units connected by
common corridors or staircases.

The most difficult type of apartment blocks in which to set the compass points are: extremely long blocks, blocks with semicircular shapes and those with irregular connections. With such designs, the magnetic field feng shui method is not applicable. This is because the many angles present within these buildings make it hard for the forces that come into the area to settle. The forces come into the buildings and slip into the irregular nooks and corners between the blocks. They eventually turn into wind and flow out of the buildings, leaving little impact on the buildings and apartments within the buildings. Thus, feng shui applications have little impact on these types of building.

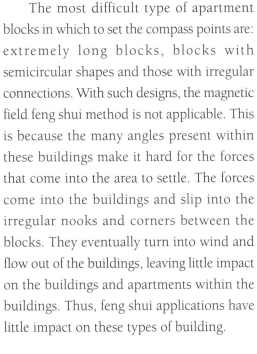

Long housing blocks like these are typical of government housing in Singapore.

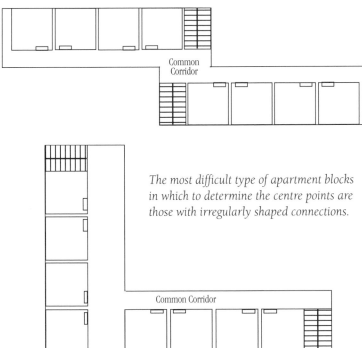

The most difficult type of apartment blocks in which to determine the centre points are those with irregularly shaped connections.

Making Changes to the Interior

The implimentation of feng shui applications into the interior of a house need not be expensive. In fact, major renovations that will incur heavy financial commitments on the part of the owner should be avoided. There are several cost efficient ways of implimenting feng shui. This includes removing and discarding worn or broken furniture, changing the colour of the walls and rearranging the furniture. The objective is to redirect the magnetic fields in order to achieve relevant feng shui effects. While rearranging the existing furniture and discarding unused furniture may not be the most effective methods, it will, however, set the fundamental principle of feng shui on its relevant path.

There are also a few important points to take note of when designing the interior of an apartment — avoid creating long corridors, placing a mirror facing the main entrance or locating the stove in front of the dining table.

There are certain feng shui principles that are constantly being applied in practical feng shui. This includes the Strike (冲), the Tight (煞), the Trap (刑) and the Harm (害). These are some of the formations created by stand-alone or cluster buildings. All contribute to causing a certain degree of harm to the environment and the building's occupants. Some effects are immediate, some may take a slightly longer period of time, while others would occur according to the workings of the individual's magnetic field. These terms are especially important when applying the

visible elements method (*Chapter 4: Practical Feng Shui*). The visible elements method emphasizes the visual impact of the layout of an environment. This is applicable to both internal and external layouts.

The Strike is the most common cause of calamity. The Strike occurs where an object such as a flag pole, a lamp post or the sharp corner of a building faces the main door or a bedroom window directly. The degree of harm caused would depend on the size and the sharpness of the object. The situation is most serious when the object points (or strikes) directly into the centre of the building's entrance or windows. If it 'strikes' to one side or into the corner, the effects may not be as harmful, although the effect may develop over time and cause the auspicious field of the door or the window to deteriorate. In time, the effects may also spread to the other related auspicious sectors within the building.

The Tight occurs when two tall buildings are built at an angle, creating a sandwiched view of the sky when one looks up from the ground level. This sandwiched space is known as the Sky-Tight (天斩煞). A tall and narrow-looking building isolated from others is known as the Brush-Tight (天笔煞). The occupants of a house facing the Sky-Tight and Brush-Tight may suffer from problems and ill health as a result of the negative forces generated by the Tight.

An overhead bridge that is angled at a building is known as the Heart-Spear (穿心

剣). If a commercial building is affected by the Heart-Spear, the economic prosperity of the shops and offices in the building would be badly affected. For domestic dwellings, the Heart-Spear is commonly a result of the pointed roof of the car porch facing into the bedroom wall. The occupants of these bedrooms may suffer from serious illnesses or poor health.

The Trap can occur both as a result of internal and external factors. When a building is surrounded by a group of larger and taller buildings to the extent that it receives little natural light, it is in a Trap. This is most common at the centre of modern cities where there are many skyscrapers. Traps also occur in the form of traffic congestions, air pollution and a generally tense atmosphere.

The Sky-Tight (天斩煞)

The Heart-Spear (穿心剑)

The pointed edge of the roof runs directly into the bedroom. The occupants of such houses usually suffer from illness and poor health.

In the interior of a building, the Trap is generally caused by clusters of furniture, doors located too close together or when there are too many turnings within a confined space. Due to the poor layout, the Trap creates a deadlock where auspicious qi cannot enter or circulate. Occupants of buildings affected by the Trap will not be able to enjoy good economic prosperity or harmonious relationships. The Harm is the conflict between the five elements of the internal sectors and the five elements of the exterior of the building. Take for example, a tall narrow building at an external northern corner of a house. According to the principles of feng shui, this northern corner belongs to the water element. The element of the tall narrow building would be wood, as it is long in shape. If the northern sector of the house is an auspicious sector, the water element will be exhausted by the wood element of the tall narrow building.

The Existing Interior

A Case Study

During one of my feng shui consultations, I visited a house that was seated west and facing east. It belonged to the western clan group. The owner of the house was born in 1950 and belonged to the western life group. Hence, both the owner and the house belonged to the same clan group. As the owner prepared to make major renovations to the house, many aspects of feng shui were taken into consideration.

The auspicious sectors of the house were northwest, west, southwest, northeast and the centre sector. The inauspicious sectors are south, east, southeast and north. The existing interior layout consisted of a number of areas which did not comply with feng shui principles. As a result of this setting, the owner was plagued with ill health. The outlook for his business dealings were also dismal. From my assessment, I found that:

1. The main gate was situated in an inauspicious sector in the southeast direction.
2. The master bedroom was situated in the auspicious sector, but the energy of this sector was absorbed by the presence of many garden plants in the northeast corner (wood conflicts with earth).
3. On the left side of the house , just outside the master bedroom, was a fountain. As the fountain was in the inauspicious north sector, the fountain became a pool of inauspiciousness.
4. The second bedroom was located in auspicious northwest sector. However, the bed and the bedroom door formed a three-point strike with the main door, causing the occupant of the room to have bad dreams and suffer from poor health and restless sleep.
5. The bed in the second bedroom, the store room door and the toilet door were visible

from the main door. The exposure of these yin elements to the yang element of the main door reduced the effects of the auspicious yang field.

6. The dining table was facing the stove directly. In feng shui, the stove is believed to generate various magnetic fields that could be negative or even poisionous. Thus, the dining table may attract and retain these negative forces if it faces the stove directly.

7. The stove (fire) was also located immediately next to the sink (water). These two conflicting elements should not be placed so close together.

8. The furniture in the sitting room was situated in the Trap, a tight corner immediately next to the toilet.

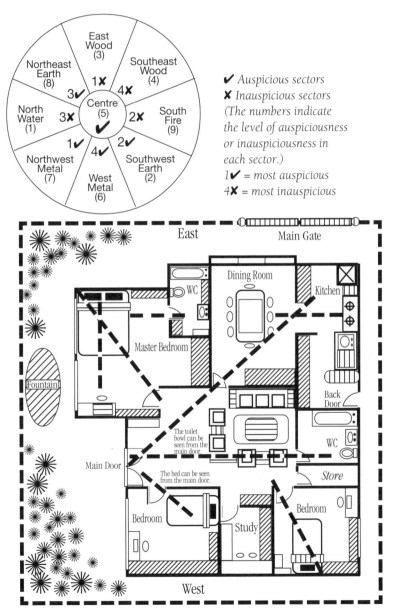

✔ Auspicious sectors
✘ Inauspicious sectors
(The numbers indicate the level of auspiciousness or inauspiciousness in each sector.)
1✔ = most auspicious
4✘ = most inauspicious

Former layout

Once the inauspicious factors were identified, steps were taken in accordance to the physical viability and cost effectiveness of each application.

1. The main gate was relocated to the auspicious northeast sector. As this sector is of the earth element, wood is a conflicting element. Hence, the plants were removed and replaced with decorative pebbles and stones. Pebbles and stones are metal elements and they act as a complementary force in this sector (earth complements metal.)

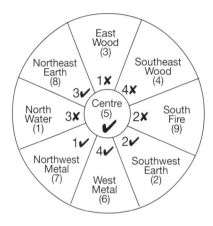

✔ *Auspicious sectors*
✘ *Inauspicious sectors*
(The numbers indicate the level of auspiciousness or inauspiciousness in each sector.)
1✔ = most auspicious
4✘ = most inauspicious

New layout

2. The master bedroom was already in the auspicious sector, though the bed had to be relocated to the west side and placed facing the east. This was an auspicious location for both the owner's life group and the house clan group.

The plants situated in the north corner outside the bedroom were reduced, not removed entirely. This is because the north sector is an inauspicious sector and the plants will reduce the inauspicious energy produced by the northern water element.

3. The fountain was removed as it was situated too close to the bed in the master bedroom. The bed was relocated to a better position following the owner's life group.

4. As the second bedroom was already located in an auspicious sector, the bed and the door were simply repositioned to avoid the three-point bed strike. The bed was moved to an auspicious sector in the west and the bedroom door was relocated so that it would not be visible from the main door.

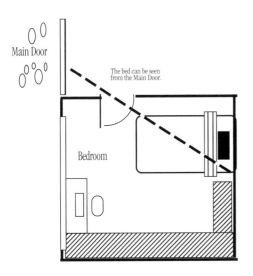

Former layout

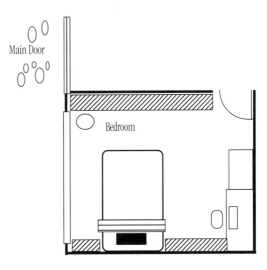

New layout

5. The storeroom was relocated to the inner section of the study. The original storeroom wall was knocked down and used as an extended bedroom. An inner partition was installed near the bed to avoid direct strikes from the toilet door. A sliding door was installed to allow access to the toilet from this bedroom. The original toilet door was relocated and replaced with a sliding door accessible from the hall to avoid the three-door strike.

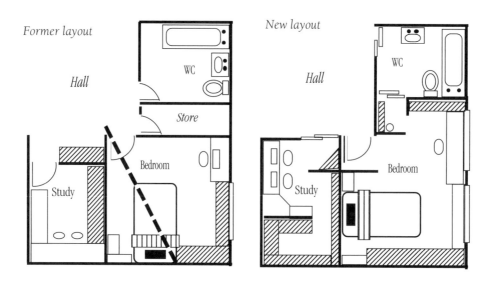

6. The kitchen door was relocated to avoid a direct strike between the stove and dining table.
7. The positions of the stove and the sink were also relocated. Two sets of indoor plants were placed between the sink and stove. This would create a complementary force for the plants (water from the sink) and the plants will in return complement the fire element of the stove.
8. To release the Tight in the sitting room, the door of the dining room was relocated.

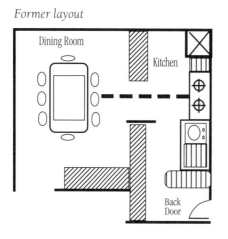

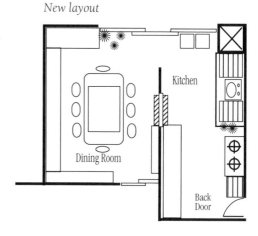

Further improvements to the house were made by creating a balcony at the front and relocating the main gate to the left of the compound. The semicircular balcony belongs to the metal element and will control the wood element in the inauspicious southeast where the main gate used to be. Some domestic plants were also placed around the balcony to stengthen the fire element in the kitchen and weaken the wood element of the inauspicious southeast.

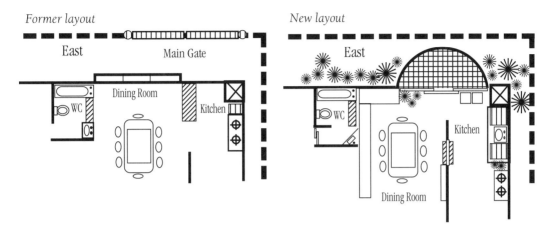

The hall in the centre of the house is an auspicious zone as the life group of the owner and the house clan group are similar. The new position of the doors and the relocation of the furniture will open up the area for qi to circulate and the Tight originally found in this section of the house will be released.

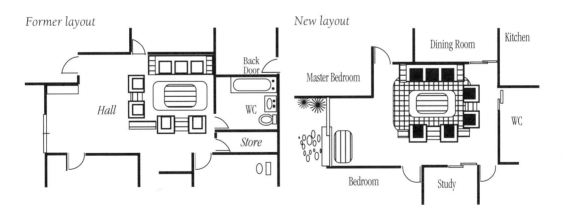

Chapter 7

Feng Shui and the Interior Part 2

The Inner Space

The majority of domestic dwellings are designed such that a person will step into the hall immediately upon entering the main door. The hall then leads the way into the other rooms and the kitchen. We have become so accustomed to this layout that if the main door leads into the kitchen or a bedroom first, it would seem unreasonable and impractical.

The main door is the main connection between the interior of the house and the exterior. With this understanding, feng shui practitioners treat the main door as the most important part of a building.

Feng shui practitioners believe that placing a prominent point of spirit (精神壁) at the sector which is immediately visible to anyone entering the front door, will enable the spirit of the house to be maintained. This spirit point will have the power to prevent unpleasant and negative forces from entering the house. It is also a centre point to maintain the harmonious relationships among the occupants. Paintings, sculptures or antiques are sometimes displayed at the prominent point of spirit of the house. This point must be kept in proper order at all times.

The prominent point of spirit must be
kept in proper order at all times.

Antiques are sometimes
placed at the prominent
point of spirit.

Sunlight, Water and Air

The most important elements for good feng shui are sunlight, water and air. Allow as much sunlight as possible into the house during the day. The interior should be bright in the day, but there should also not be too much reflection from walls or floor tiles which could cause the occupants to suffer from eye problems and migraines. To reduce glare and reflection, hanging paintings on the walls and using floor mats may help.

The availability of water contributes to good health and hygiene and a good flow of air means that qi will be well-circulated throughout the house.

The house must be filled with as much natural light as possible during the day.

Doors

The three major items to bear in mind when doing up the interior of a house are the doors, beds and kitchen stove. In this section, we will discuss the topic of doors.

In feng shui, doors are very important as they are the 'mouth' of the house or building. Qi enters and leaves through them. For a house to have good feng shui, the size of the main door must not be larger than that of the main gate.

The bedroom door must also be a single leaf door and it must be smaller in size than that of the main door. The size of the storeroom and toilet doors may generally be of the same size as the bedroom doors. As for the cupboard or wardrobe doors, they must be smaller than the doors of the rooms.

Room doors are generally single leaf doors whereas the main door should be double leaf doors if possible. As the main door leads to the exterior of the building, having double leaf doors creates an impression of welcome when they are opened. Most modern dwellings are built with single leaf main doors. According to feng shui principles, living in an apartment with a single leaf main door may be likened to being confined to a bedroom. The qi that enters the building is confined and isolated. It develops into a negative force and will cause the breakdown of relationships among the occupants.

As a solution, an additional double leaf metal gate may be installed at the front entrance. This would give the same

Type of Doors

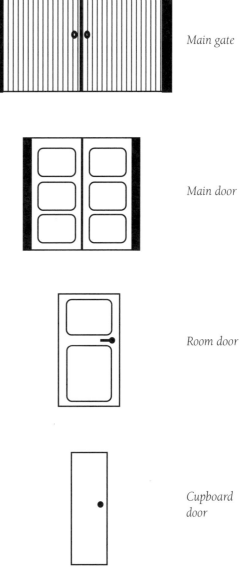

Main gate

Main door

Room door

Cupboard door

impression of open arms and of welcome. When installing double leaf doors, however, the two leaves must be of an equal size. Some gates are bigger on one side and they are commercially referred to as 'Mother and Child' or 'Prosperity' doors. These are simply commercial gimmicks and such doors will instead bring about disharmony between the old and young living within the building.

Most doors are either made of wood or metal today. As these are the two main materials used for doors, only the colours and shape of the doors need to be considered when applying the principles of the five elements in assessing doors.

While doors may be square, rectangular or circular, it would not be practical for them to be triangular or irregular in shape. These shapes of the five elements may instead be applied as patterns on the door.

The effect of the five element complementary force on homes will depend on how the elements are applied. For example, if a main door is situated in the east, the element that would bring energy would be water. The colour for water is black and its geometrical form is an irregular shape. The door can thus be painted in tones of black and decorated with irregular patterns if desired. Some shades of green may also be added as green complements black. The application of colours and their respective geometrical forms can also be applied to the external walls of the building. As with all feng shui applications, however, practicality should always be considered.

The main door should ideally be a double leaf door.

Doors may be square, rectangular or circular.

A double leaf metal gate where the left and right leaves are of equal size.

Most people fix coat hangers or hooks onto the back of bedroom doors. While there is nothing wrong with this practice, it must be noted that metal screws or nails must not be knocked into wooden doors as metal conflicts with wood. Coat hangers should instead be fixed onto concrete or brick walls behind the door as concrete or brick walls belong to the earth element which complements metal. If the wall is made of wood, however, then this is not advisable. An alternative would be to use a floor hanger.

Today, most doors also have metal hinges and locks and this cannot be avoided. The use of these metal elements, however, should be kept to a minimum.

A main door that looks directly into the back of the house would also mean that any qi entering the house would not have time to circulate into the other areas before it travels straight out the back of the house. In such cases, a partition may be erected as a barrier to separate the main door from the back.

A partition is built at the front door to avoid direct vision into the back of the house from the main door.

Coat hangers should be fixed on the concrete or brick wall behind the door.

Stoves

The heat from the kitchen stove has the power to drive away negative and inauspicious forces. As such, it should be placed within the inauspicious sectors of the house. It is also important to ensure that the stove is stable and not prone to rock or shake. The stove is where most of the meals are cooked each day. Thus, it contributes to the health of everyone who consumes food cooked with it. It is believed that a shaky stove will cause unrest and poor health in the home. The stove must also not be moved too often for the purpose of cleaning. It should stand in a fixed position. The following points are to be observed in using and maintaining a stove.

1. Do not hit or drop any heavy cooking utensils on top of the stove.
2. Do not cut or chop food on top of the stove.
3. Do not place any electrical appliances on the stove.
4. Do not place any tools (hammer, screw driver, knife or scissors) on the stove.
5. Never splash large amounts of water on the stove when cleaning it.
6. Do not leave any food on the stove overnight. The stove must be cleaned and cleared after the last meal of the day has been prepared.
7. Keep the kitchen tidy, especially the area near the stove.
8. Do no place the stove under sewage pipes.

Beds

A person spends an average of 30 percent of his entire life sleeping. Sleep enables the body to recharge lost energy. The bed is like a battery charger that recharges one's physical energy at an interval of every 16–18 hours. Throughout the day, apart from the time used to consume food and drink, energy is continuously being used and exhausted. The bed must thus be placed at an auspicious sector to ensure that auspicious forces are circulated during the recharging process. The following points are to be observed in the placement and treatment of the bed.

1. The mattress must be replaced every three to five years regardless of its condition. This is based on the fact that the ideal life span for the standard mattress is about three years. After three years, the quality of the mattress begins to deteriorate due to the presence of germs and dust.

2. Similarly, all pillows must also be replaced after three to five years of use.

3. The bed must be located where there is a good circulation of air and where sunlight shines in during the day.

4. Avoid placing the bed near a window on the western side of the room where it will catch the rays of the setting sun.

5. Do not store anything such as carton boxes, plastic bags or suitcases under the bed.

6. Do not fix any overhead lights immediately over the bed. Move them to the side or fix them on the wall instead. The ceiling immediately over the bed must be kept clear of fixtures.

7. All permanent occupants of a household must have a permanent bed at a fixed location. Sleeping on the floor with a foldable mattress on a permanent basis is not encouraged.

8. Do not cover the bed with a blanket or bedspread immediately after rising. Leave it uncovered for at least 30 minutes each time before making the bed.

... A number of positions
to avoid placing the bed are shown
in the following pages.

Positioning the Bed — The Strikes

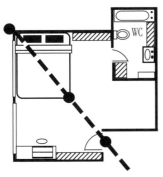

The three-point strike :
This is when two corners of the bed form a straight line with the door.

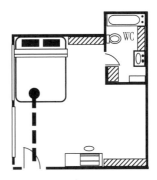

The direct strike :
This is when the bed is placed facing the door directly.

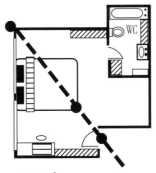

The three-point strike :
In this case, the strike is created by one corner of the room, one corner of the bed and the door forming a straight line.

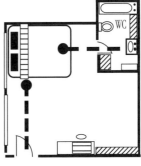

The side-strike :
This is when one side of the bed runs directly into the door.

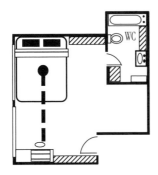

The object-strike :
The bed directly faces a large object such as wardrobe, table, large mirror, large picture frame or sculptures.

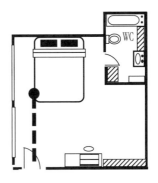

The side strike :
This is when one side of the bed runs directly into the door.

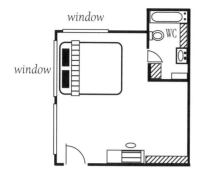

window

window

Positioning the Bed —
Emptiness

Do not place the bed in a corner such that a triangular space is created at the head. It does not make a difference whether or not there are triangular storage shelves fitted into the space.

The external strikes:
Do not place the bed next to windows especially when large objects or the corners of buildings are visible from the window.

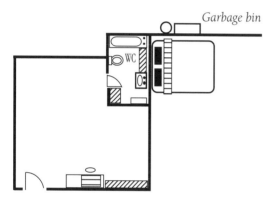

Garbage bin

WC

Do not place the bed next to where the wash basin or toilet bowl are located in the next room or where the garbage bin is situated outside the house.

Do not place the bed such that there is a gap at the head.

Do not place the bed in the middle of the room.

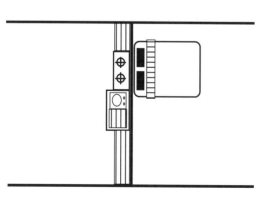

Do not place the bed next to where the kitchen sink or stove is located in the next room.

Positioning the Bed — Vibrations

Do not place the bed behind a partition or a cupboard.

Altar table

Do not place the bed behind an altar table or large statues even if it is on the other side of the wall.

Hi-fi systems

Do not place the bed behind hi-fi systems even if it is on the other side of the wall.

Positioning the Bed — External Strikes

Do not place the bed where there is a big tree immediately on the other side of the wall.

Do not place the bed immediately next to a carpark or park any vehicle next to where the bed is on the other side of the wall.

Fountain or fish pond.

Do not place the bed where there is a fountain or fish pond on the other side of the wall.

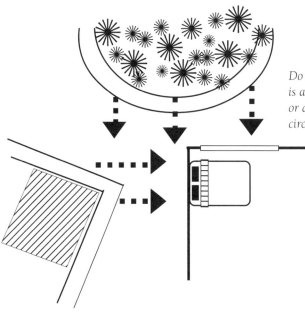

Do not place the bed in a position where there is a major circular road, a river, a roundabout or any other feature that faces inward in a circular or pointed manner.

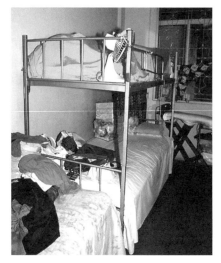

Do not use the bed for storage purposes.

Do not display weapons in the bedroom.

Do not place the bed too near electronic systems that contain magnetic elements.

A partition can block the door strikes from any door affecting the bed.

Bedrooms

The bedroom is a very complex environment today. Apart from the extra large sized bed, there are other items that have found their way into the bedroom. They include plants, large mirrors, televisions, hi-fi sets, karaoke systems, bar fridges and even shoe racks.

Here are some points to take note of when doing up the bedroom.

1. Plants, whether real or artificial, are not suitable to be placed in the bedroom and especially in children's bedrooms. Live plants absorb oxygen and give out carbon dioxide at night. This is not advised for health reasons. Artificial plants, on the other hand, collect dust and may cause the occupant to fall ill.

2. Avoid putting any electronic devices such as televisions or hi-fi systems in the bedroom as they produce negative forces even when they are not in use. For those who enjoy the convenience, however, the following points should be observed:

- Use only smaller sets of any electronic devices and place them as far away from the bed as possible.

- For a room size of up to 25 sq m (5x5 m), the television screen size should not exceed 15 inches. It should also be placed on a higher plane or at the furthest corner of the room away from the bed.

- To dissolve the negative forces generated by the television, place some crystals, mineral rocks or natural pebbles in front of the television set. It is also advisable to use a radiation-free television screen shield.

3. Large mirrors are not suitable to be placed in the bedroom because the qi created is too powerful for the sleeping occupant. The ideal place for the mirror in the bedroom is inside the wardrobe door.

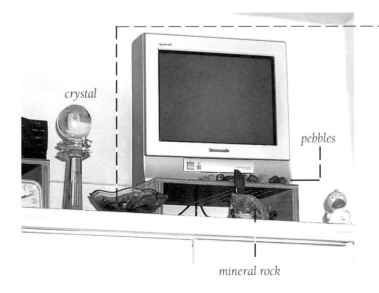

crystal

pebbles

mineral rock

Place the television set on top of a shelf at least 3 m away from the bed. Display natural stones such as crystals, mineral rocks or natural pebbles in front of the set to dissolve the negative forces.

The ideal place for the mirror is inside the wardrobe door.

Place the television set as far away from the bed as possible.

Storage Areas

It is a common habit to keep old or broken furniture in the storeroom, in the belief that the furniture might become useful again some day. Most of the time, however, the unused furniture tends to be forgotten. It is also common to store excess cutlery, pots and other cooking utensils in the kitchen, thinking that they might come in handy some day. Often, much of the available space in a house is taken up by broken furniture, old television sets, old mattresses, old shoes, souvenirs, artificial flowers and boxes.

In the practice of feng shui, it is believed that these objects would have a negative effect on the auspicious energy of the house. As a result of long periods of storage, the qi in the furniture deteriorates and may conflict with the qi in other objects. This will overide all the auspicious elements of feng shui originally applied in the house. It is thus advisable to discard any clothing or shoes not worn for more than six months. Do not develop the habit of storing too many new or unused items either. This inlcudes defective electrical appliances. Send them for repair or discard them.

Faulty or broken fixtures and furniture such as doors, windows, cupboards, electrical cables and pipes must be attended to immediately. Do not store objects in large plastic bags and leave them on top of or behind cupboards and shelves, underneath beds or behind the bedroom doors. The circulation of positive qi within areas of storage is lower and will result in the development of negative zones.

Do not use the top of cupboards and shelves as storage areas.

The storage areas are the negative zones of the house.

Artificial Lighting

Artificial lighting is the most important source of light after sunlight. There are many different types of lighting used in homes today. In general, they can be classified as cool and warm lights. Cool lights are those that do not produce heat. Examples of this category of lights are fluorescent and ultraviolet lights. Warm lights are those that produce heat such as standard light bulbs and spot lights. They are considered as having yang elements close to that of sunlight.

In cooler climates, most households use warm lights which give a warm and cosy feel to the house. In tropical climates, fluorescent lights are more commonly used. However, it is advisable that domestic dwellings utilise warm positive lights.

Besides the bedrooms, dining room and sitting room, the other rooms that would benefit from the installation of warm lights are the toilets and the storerooms. Warm lights help increase the yang element and reduce the yin forces in these rooms. These lights should be at least 60 watts. The ideal voltage would be 100 watts. In houses where there are long corridors and many small nooks and corners, warm lights should be used as much as possible.

The different forms of warm lights.

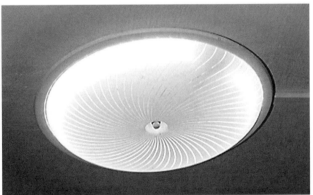

The long and round
flourescent tubes are
cool lights.

Aquariums

Feng shui practitioners believe that having fish tanks in the home is a prosperity generator. Aquariums may be placed in any auspicious sector of the house, except for the bedrooms, storeroom and toilets. In setting up an aquarium for feng shui purposes, there are certain aspects to pay attention to, including the number and types of fish as well as the set-up of the tank.

Types of fish

The most favoured type of fish for the purpose of feng shui is the carp (koi). Carps may be reared in ponds sited at auspicious locations in the garden. They may be reared with other types of fish such as goldfish. It is auspicious to have nine carps in a pond. The best combination is one white carp and eight red ones. Both these numbers (one and eight) are considered to be auspicious and the total number that they make up — nine — is the heavenly number.

Indoors, the more auspicious variety of fishes are goldfish, discus, angel fish and red parrots. Red parrots are known as the feng shui fish as they are very sensitive to environmental changes. The type of forces

circulating indoors are reflected in the colour and appearance of the red parrots. In an environment with positive forces, the red parrots will maintain their bright red colour and generally respond to strangers with a friendly or carefree appearance. In an environment with negative forces, the red parrots will take on a pale colour and will be nervous in their movements.

For goldfish, discus and red parrots, it is auspicious to have them in combinations of one and six. This refers to having one black and six red fishes of the same species. Other auspicious numerical combinations are one and eight or one and nine. Alternatively, you may have these fishes all in one colour in even numbers with the exception of the heavenly number, nine. Different species may be kept together in an aquarium or pond, if each species makes up for its own number. Odd numbers are inauspicious with the exception of the numbers one and nine.

Fishes such as the arowana (also considered a feng shui fish, but are more suited for offices and factories), oscars and other fish that feed on live bait are not suitable for keeping in domestic dwellings. This is due to their propensity to 'kill' and 'destroy' life.

Locations for the Aquarium

There are a few locations where the domestic aquarium should not be placed even if it is in the auspicious sector.

1. Do not place the aquarium opposite a stove. If it is placed on the left or right side of the stove, place an indoor plant between them.

2. Do not place the aquarium facing or underneath any religious artifacts such as an altar table or pictures of gods.

3. Do not place the aquarium at a location where it is visible from the bed. Never put an aquarium in the bedroom.

4. For double storey apartments, do not place the aquarium where there is a bed or a bedroom on the floor above.

Red parrots are known as the feng shui fish.

Angel fish are auspicious fish. It is auspicious to have eight angel fish.

Wind Chimes

The sound of the wind chime has the ability to mobilise stagnant magnetic fields. It can be placed in either the auspicious or inauspicious sectors of the house. It has the ability to stabilise and balance pleasant and unpleaseant forces.

There is a saying that wind chimes attract evil forces or, in layman terms, it attracts ghosts — it creates a door for the devil to enter the house. I believe, however, that the devil or ghosts will enter houses with or without the wind chime, if the fundamental principles of feng shui for the house are not observed.

Wind chimes come in various forms. A good wind chime is one that produces a clear and sleek sound that resounds in every corner of the room. Wind chimes made from shells or clay are not ideal as they do not meet this requirement.

The number of tubes in a wind chime is not of particular importance, but it can generally be based on the numerical principles of feng shui. Five tubes are suitable for general purposes, four tubes are to enforce study forces and three tubes are for drawing prosperity. Wind chimes with four tubes are suitable for the study room while those with three or five tubes would be suitable for the main hall or sitting room.

Wind chimes that come in the form of a single bell can be used for all purposes. It is advisable to fix up the wind chime on an auspicious day.

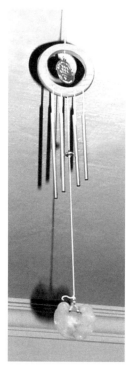

Wind chimes come in various forms. A good wind chime is one with a clear and sleek sound.

Crystals

Crystals are considered to be one of the most auspicious items in the practice of feng shui. They are generators of prosperity and have the ability to dissolve negative magnetive forces and stabilise the magnetic fields in any environment. They can be located at either the auspicious or inauspicious sectors.

The best form of crystals are the raw and untreated type. Most commercially available crystals have been refined for display purposes. Crystals, especially those selected from a commercial retailer, must be purified under running water for a minimum of 72 hours (3 days). On the fourth day before dawn, place the crystal on the ground in the garden where it can have direct contact with the earth and leave it there for a minimum of two to six hours. Alternatievly, just place the crystal at the display point after 72 hours of water purification. Do not move the crystal unnecessarily or allow anyone to handle it after it has been purified and positioned.

Commercial crystals are refined in appearance.

The purple coloured raw crystal is a good crystal. Position it with the longest point facing the north.

This is a raw crystal I found in Kota Kinabaru. I named it The Palm.

Natural stones, apart from being decorative pieces, can work to balance the forces indoors.

A mini sculpture of a man deep in thought is flanked by two natural patterned slabs from Inner Mongolia, China.

The Dragon Dance, a crystal from Taiwan.

The Immortal, a red rock from Taiwan.

Pebbles depicting birth signs and the yin and yang elements.

Point of Prosperity

The point of prosperity is one of the locations in the home that most people would be excited about. If located correctly, the home owner will gain prosperity. The point of prosperity was never clearly indicated in the historical records of feng shui, but it has been developed and practised by the majority of feng shui practitioners in recent years.

The point of prosperity must not be disturbed once it has been positioned. There are a number of objects that are generally placed at this point, including crystals, natural mineral rocks and miniature Chinese zodiac animals that bring luck to the owner. Inauspicious objects such as brooms, dust pans, garbage bins, dirty laundry, rags and broken objects must not be located near or at the point of prosperity.

The most common location for the point of prosperity would be the northeast sector of the house. This sector is associated with the auspicious number eight. In Chinese numerology, the number eight is also a symbol of prosperity. It may not always be practical, however, to develop the northeast sector into a prosperity point. In certain houses, there could be a toilet, staircase, kitchen or storeroom situated in the northeast sector. In such cases, this point cannot be developed. An alternative point would have to be located.

Other locations that have been referred to as the point of prosperity are the points located at about 45° from the immediate left and right hand corners of the main door. This would, however, only be possible if the main door is centrally located along the front of the house. If it is not centralised, only the left or right corner may be considered.

When locating the point of prosperity in a multi-storey apartment, ensure that the apartment on the floor just above does not have a toilet, bedroom, storeroom or kitchen located at the same point. As these are considered the yin points of a building, they might 'burden' the point of prosperity if it is located directly below.

The northeast sector is considered to be the point of prosperity.

Southeast 4 Xun	South 9 Li	Southwest 2 Kun
East 3 Zhen	The Centre Zone	West 7 Dui
Northeast 8 Gen	North 1 Kan	Northwest 6 Qian

The immediate left and right hand corners from the main door may be considered to be the point of prosperity.

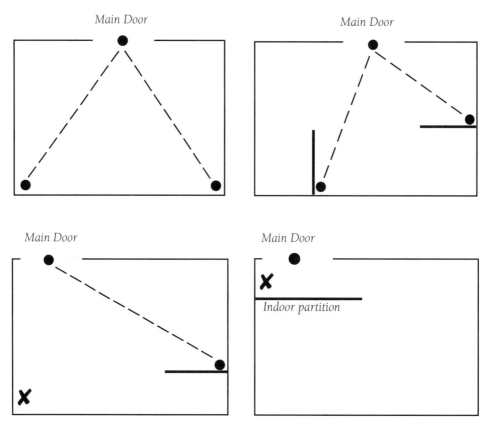

If the main door is not centralised, there is only one point of prosperity.

There is no available point in this layout.

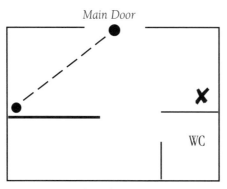

A point next to the toilet cannot be considered as a point of prosperity.

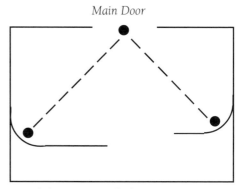

Rounded corners are the best prosperity points.

Auspicious objects such as mineral rocks, coins, crystals, the abacus and statues of the goddess of prosperity may be arranged at the point of prosperity.

A family of one sow and six piglets is located on the bottom shelf. The auspicious figures of one and six resemble the water element. Water symbolises wealth .

Chapter 8

Haunted House

A haunted house is one that is believed to be occupied by unnatural forces, or in other words, *ghosts*. I have always believed that ghosts are negative forces that enter the human consciousness at places where the environmental forces are negative. These forces are strongest when you have a guilty conscience against your ego force. To further explain the importance that feng shui plays in a domestic dwelling, I would like to share with you my personal encounter with ghosts.

As a feng shui consultant for the Tam Kung Temple in Sandakan, Sabah, East Malaysia, I visit Sabah at least once a year to provide feng shui services to the locals. I usually make a stopover at Kota Kinabaru, a city approximately 30 minutes away by plane from Sandakan. Here, I would often stay over at the apartment of one of my students.

As it was a rental apartment, it was not properly maintained. There was a lot of old furniture stacked all the way from the front of the apartment, right into the kitchen and backyard. There were also many unused items stacked near the doorway and along the staircase leading to the second floor where the bedrooms were. Moving around in the apartment was difficult as 80 percent of the

floor space was taken up by these items. At the top of the staircase was the guestroom where I stayed. There were Taoist talismans on every door including the toilet door in the guestroom. As the use of talismans is common among the people of Sabah, I did not pay much attention to them.

In the guestroom, it was my habit to place my luo pan upright on a stand, together with a black paper fan, that had the Buddhist sutra printed on it, on the writing table facing the bed. I left them there for the first three nights I was there. On the last evening of my visit, however, I packed my luggage and put the luo pan and the paper fan into a bag.

When I turned off the lights and was ready to go to sleep, all of a sudden, I felt someone forcing a plank of wood into my back, in an effort to throw me out of bed. Following that, I felt two hands grabbing the waist of my trousers and trying to force it up towards my face, as if it were trying to cover my face with it. After the sudden jolt from the plank, I had already prepared myself for a second encounter. As soon as I felt that it was trying to cover my face with my trousers, I bent my knees towards my waist hoping to hit this *thing*. However, as I was bending my knees upward, a hand caught my right leg and tried to pull it back. I could feel five fingers on my ankle. All these happened within a few seconds and in total darkness. Fear began to overcome me. Then I thought of closing my palms and raising them to my head in order to create a circular flow of energy from my palms to my mind. This energy flow would stabilise my concentration and help me work out a way to overcome any more attacks from this *thing*. I was at the same time preparing to chant a Buddhist sutra as soon as I was in position. However, this *thing* seemed to have read my thoughts and my shoulders were locked by some strange forces. I was paralysed! I was not able to chant the sutra either because my throat was clamped by two fingers.

It was not until this moment that my fear began to turn into anger. Knowing that it could read my thoughts, I began to confuse it by coming up with a chain of wild and unrelated thoughts. I eventually managed to confuse the *thing* and it was during this time that I began to chant and my shoulders were loosened. I sat up on the bed with both palms closed. I was very angry by that time and I began to chant a complete Buddhist sutra and warned this thing that I could chant more destructive sutras. I asked it to leave me alone and I tried to go to sleep. Just before I closed my eyes, I could feel that it was coming back again. I decided to unpack my luo pan and put it back on the table. I also chanted the sutra three times. After that, I warned the thing that if it came again, I would continue to chant throughout the night. Then I went

back to bed, taking the black fan with me. That ended the horrific confrontation with the *thing*.

In the morning, my student said he heard a commotion coming from my room during the night. In order not to scare the household, I told him that I was not aware.

The following year, I was again invited to Kota Kinabaru for a consultation. I asked my student to book a hotel room for me this time, but he said that he had prepared the same room for me. With no valid reason to turn down his offer, I accepted, reluntantly.

That night, I could not decide if I should sleep in the bed or on the floor, but I was sure that I needed a good night's rest. I decided to negotiate with the *thing*, although I could not be certain if it still existed. Nevertheless, I told it that it could have the bed. I would sleep on the floor, but I would take the mattress. With no certainty of any agreement from the *thing*, I left my luo pan on the table pointing in the direction where I was to sleep and carried the black fan with me before stepping onto the mattress. Suddenly, something pulled my hand, causing me to fall. I asked it to take the bed and leave me alone. There was no further confrontation.

That same year, my student moved to a new house. I decided then to tell him about my encounters. He revealed that no one had ever been able to spend a peaceful night in that guestroom.

Today, whenever I travel to Sabah, I would check into a hotel as I do not wish to test my ability to confront negative forces.

The haunted guestroom

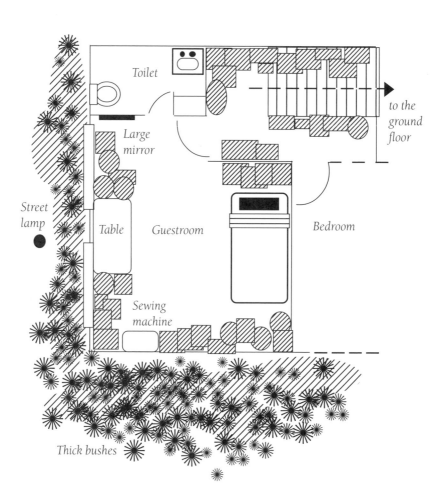

to the
ground
floor

Toilet

Large
mirror

Street
lamp

Table

Guestroom

Bedroom

Sewing
machine

Thick bushes

⊘▨ *Carton boxes and plastic bags*

Upon reflection, I believe that the guestroom was haunted because:

1. The house was packed with too many unnecessary objects.
2. The staircase was very cluttered, leaving only about one third of it free.
3. The guestroom doubled up as a storeroom when there were no guests.
4. There were too many talismans around, causing visitors to react negatively to them.
5. A lamp post directly outside the bedroom window was visible from the bed .
6. There was an unused sewing machine in one corner of the room with a lot of excess fabric around it. Underneath the machine, there were about six boxes of old shoes.
7. The garden was overgrown and full of wild bushes. Next to it was a narrow side road about 2 m from the house.
8. The bed was placed with a gap between it and the wall. In this gap was a number of bags storing unused items. Underneath the bed, there were a few carton boxes.
9. Next to the toilet door, there was a large mirror that was very reflective because there was a window next to it .

Learning from my experience, homeowners should be aware of the negative forces that may result from careless placement of items and from external factors.

The Haunted Environment

A haunted environment usually develops from the presence of negative forces. Generally, this is a result of the original land conditions, but it can also be caused by human negligence. In our living environment, it is vital to maintain all elements within the positive forces. This includes giving consideration to the nine numbers, the use of colour and psychological effects.

In this case, the positive numbers are the odd numbers and the negative numbers are the even numbers. For example, in following the principle of the positive numbers, a house should have three, five, seven or nine rooms although the practical number would be three rooms. This does not include the storeroom, kitchen or dining room. Apartments with more than three bedrooms would mean that there are either too many people living under one roof or that the unoccupied rooms would be converted into guestrooms. And when there are no guests, these rooms usually end up as some form of a storeroom.

Storerooms and unoccupied rooms are places that will easily become haunted. This is due to the development of static magnetic forces when there is no contact with positive forces from humans. When the static forces turn negative, they will cause an extreme biophysical reaction. The weaker forces may cause the occupants of the house to suffer long term, periodical or sudden illness and poor academic performance. The stronger forces may cause the occupants to suffer from migraines, strokes and heart attacks. In extreme cases, they may even cause sudden death. The negative forces in these rooms may also have developed from a combination of other negative forces from external sources. This could be due to the presence of insects or other animals that died near the house. These external negative forces can enter through air-vents, windows and wall cracks.

Industrial waste buried in nearby grounds or a graveyard located on higher ground near the area could also contribute to the building up of negative forces. Other related possibilities are deaths that may have taken place in the rooms or that the rooms could have been used by a sick or mentally ill person for a long period of time previously. When these negative forces come in contact with the stagnant forces in the rooms, the rooms will gradually become haunted. This will also happen to the whole house if it is not occupied for a long period of time.

These stagnant negative forces in the rooms are easily attracted to positive forces especially from humans. In such situations, they may speed towards the human body at the moment when the positive human forces are lowered, when the person is falling asleep. There are times when these forces move in only after the person has fallen into deep sleep. The person may then suffer from nightmares or may even die while asleep.

Maintaining the Positive Forces

Positive forces are developed through the individual's lifestyle, mode of thinking and the relationships one has with the immediate environment. Should physical health and daily living routines be overlooked from time to time, this may result in the deterioration of the positive forces.

Different levels of negative and positive forces exist. They may vary within the hour, day, month and year, or from room to room. They even exist in food, clothing and all the things that we use or come into contact with daily. However, the most important forces are the psychological encounters that remain in the inner mind, in balance with the ego forces.

Positive forces can only be developed through positive thinking and this is affected by the differences among the many things that are within or around the individual. Psychological balances between the individual and the environment will also depend on influencers of the ego such as religion and social contacts. Most sincere religious followers have stronger positive forces that enable them to have the upper hand when they encounter unforeseen negative forces. People who are religious have developed within themselves a positive force, which in most cases, will prevent negative ego forces from growing. Whatever the circumstances, never try to investigate or examine a place believed to be haunted. People have varying levels of magnetic fields and as such, not everyone will meet up with the same level of negative forces or be able to counter them in the same way.

Negative Grounds

The application of feng shui principles will have little impact on a house or apartment situated near or on negative grounds. Negative areas include graveyards, swamps, triangular plots of land, industrial zones, power stations, hospitals, military camps, prisons, schools and warehouses. Within a house or apartment, it is also not advisable to have room partitions that isolate a triangular space. Negative forces may develop in these areas due to the unbalanced flow of energies within the space.

Houses built on or situated near triangular plots of land may become haunted due to the unbalanced flow of qi.

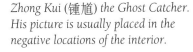

Zhong Kui (锺馗) the Ghost Catcher. His picture is usually placed in the negative locations of the interior.

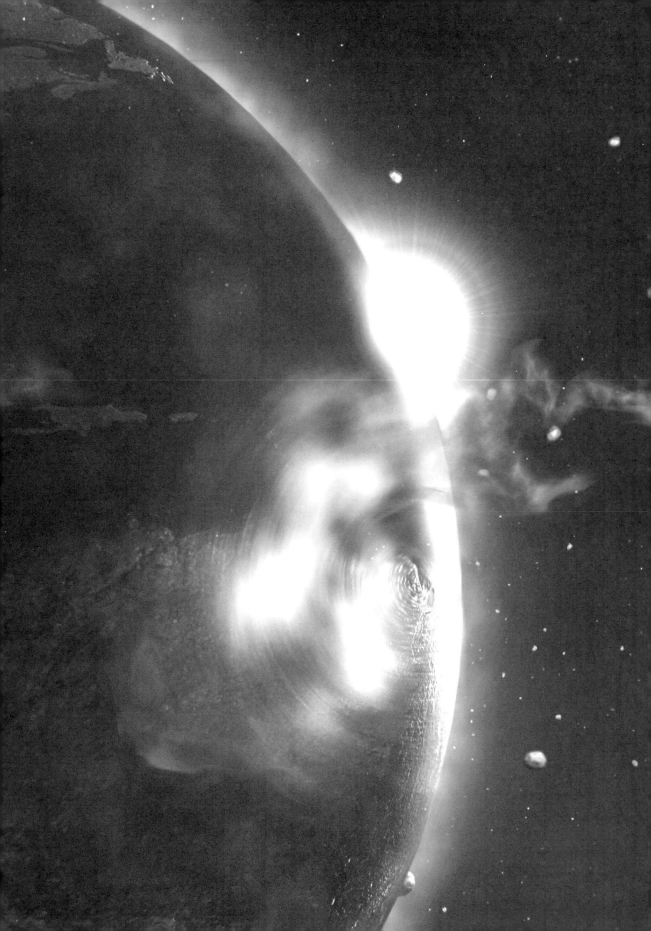

Appendix
Frequently Asked Questions

In this section, I have given answers to some common questions people have about feng shui and about my practice. Should you have more specific queries, however, please write to me via my website at www.geomancer.net.

Q1. Which clan of geomancy do you belong to?

I have studied different clan methods from a number of feng shui masters. Some of these methods cater specially to domestic dwellings while others are for business environments. Some concentrate on a person's fate in search of the appropriate method of divination, while some would concentrate on the magnetic field or flying stars theology. Some are inclined towards Taoism (spiritual method) while others are inclined towards Buddhism (Xuan Kong). I also understudied Dr. Li Heng Lih. It was then that I began to study the methods recorded in the Chinese Imperial Encyclopedia (Si Ku Quan Shu). In essence, I do not limit myself to any clan of geomancy. I base my divination according to the best method for each individual case that I assess.

Q2. How do I know if feng shui will work for me?

Feng shui works for everyone. It only depends on how long the different effects take to come about. This will vary among people, locations and the context of each situation. It is also very much dependent on the sincerity of the individual towards the feng shui application as different expectations will reap different results. Sometimes the results may take effect within hours while at other times, it could take months or even years. In the case of burial ground feng shui, the effects may not be evident until a few generations later.

Q3. How do I know if I need to change the feng shui of my house?

Usually, if you are comfortable with your current living environment, then it may not be wise to try and use feng shui in the hope of making it better, as the effects may sometimes be worse. If you consult a good feng shui practitioner, he will not force you to change your environment unless there are certain bad forces that are beginning to develop in your home. The feng shui master will then try to stop the situation from worsening.

Q4. When is the best time for a feng shui consultation for my home?

Anytime is a good time, especially when you feel that you need one. Remember, however, that the effects may not always turn out for the better.

Q5. What does a consultation include and how long does a session take?

I do not usually conduct consultations, but some of my students do. In special circumstances, I would need at least two hours. Depending on the situation at hand, I will try to explain to my clients what I am doing and why. The two-hour session will probably include the process of locating the various points of positive forces and in the case of a home, the ideal positioning of the stove, beds and toilets. I will also advise my clients on the most suitable time for a renovation, if it is needed, or the alternative measures to take for more difficult situations, such as when a toilet is located at the wrong place and cannot be repositioned.

Q6. What do I need to know if the floor area of my new apartment is small?

The application of feng shui to modern apartments is sometimes impractical because of the general layout of the building. To apply feng shui to apartments, you may have to consider the whole block instead of just one unit. Hence, the benefits that result will be shared among all the occupants in the block. This could be as many as 100 households (*see Chapter 6: Feng Shui and the Interior – Part 1*). There are, however, a few important points to observe in order to enhance the feng shui of your individual unit:

1. Allow for natural light and a good flow of air (not strong wind) in all rooms.
2. Ensure that there is minimal reflection from the floors and wall tiles.
3. Furniture and fixtures should not occupy more than 60 percent of the total floor area of the apartment. At least 40 percent of each room should be kept free.
4. Avoid buying bulky furniture and appliances since your apartment is small.

Q7. How do I assess if a property has good feng shui before purchasing it?

You can begin by taking note of the surroundings. The front of the property should not be blocked by large and tall buildings or trees. There should also not be too much reflection from the glass windows of surrounding buildings or strong lighting from the opposite directions. Other practical factors should also be considered. The property should be easily accessible to and from your home and workplace. The surrounding amenities should also offer convenience and suit your lifestyle. As for the interior of the property, it must have a good flow of air. Once these points are met, you can then consider the magnetic field feng shui principles and directions, and their relationship with yours and your family's birth dates.

Q8. I share an apartment with some friends. Where should I place the ba gua?

When a ba gua is needed for an apartment, it is generally placed above the main door. This is regardless of the number of family members or individuals sharing the apartment. Do note that the ba gua must not be placed in the bedrooms, toilet or kitchen. It is, however, acceptable in the study or the sitting room, though it must not be placed facing any bedroom door, toilet or portraits of people.

The Author

C.P. Lim holds a Masters degree in Visual Communications and was formerly the director of the School of Visual Arts at an art institution in Singapore. He has held the vice presidency of the Society of Taoist Philosophy Studies in Singapore since 1995. He is also a member of the International Institute of Tao Philosophy in Taiwan.

C.P. Lim's interest in fate and theological studies began in his school days, but it was only later in his life that he became a disciple of Dr. Li Heng Lih (李亨利博士), an I-Ching, Five Schools Studies and Oriental Cultural professor (五术与中华文化哲学教授) from Taiwan. Under the tutelage of Dr. Li Heng Lih, C.P. Lim mastered I-Ching, fate and fortune studies, appellation, theological studies, the philosophy of Lao Zi and Zhuang Zi, the principles of the Art of War and Tao culture.

Amongst the various subjects in Taoist philosophy, fate studies and Tao culture, C.P. Lim's focus is in geomancy, the principles of enviromental forces. He has been invited to conduct many lectures on geomancy, architecture, interior and environmental design principles in many countries, but most frequently in Singapore, Malaysia and China.

C.P. Lim has published a number of visual communications design and I-Ching related articles and geomancy books. *The Science of Feng Shui* is his first book written in English.

This photograph was taken on a feng shui study trip led by Dr. Li Heng Lih at Hua Mountain in China.

Index

The Science of Feng Shui